Ron Scheese is exceptionally gifted both as a leader and as a human being. He has dealt with every situation imaginable with compassion, wisdom, and appropriate firmness. As CEO of Andesa Services, he is held by the Board, its employees, and its clients to the highest standards imaginable. The reader will profit very much from reading his story in this book.

—**John E. Walker,** *Founder, Andesa Services*

The preoccupation of any effective leader should be the establishment and development of an internal culture—one that is healthy and vibrant. I've had the privilege of working with many of the most effective leaders in the world as a teacher and student of leadership. In my experience, there are few examples of effective leadership more compelling than the work of John Walker and Ron Scheese at Andesa. In *More Than a Company,* Ron offers real world insights and stories about the importance of values in driving the relationships which benefit the entire ecosystem. I highly recommend this book to anyone who is interested in leadership.

—**Kevin Graham Ford,** *Chief Catalyst, Leighton Ford Ministries; Coauthor,* The Secret Sauce: Creating a Winning Culture *and* The Leadership Triangle

This is not your typical "how-to" business book. Scheese shares his leadership journey at Andesa Services, an employee-owned company, and provides real world examples of how a values-driven company creates a powerful ecosystem of relationships among both employees and customers to build a successful, enduring business.

—**Wendy York,** *Dean, Wilbur O. and Ann Powers College of Business, Clemson University; Board member, Andesa Services*

Andesa is a unique company with a great team built around a solid set of values. Ron Scheese captures the essence of what it means to lead and inspire a team to place the company's values at the center of what they do every day. This is an uplifting example of transformational leadership.

—**Charles "Rip" Tilden,** *Partner, Makarios Consulting; Coauthor,* Leading on Purpose; *Board Chair, Andesa Services*

Ron Scheese has captured the essence of a values-based leadership culture. His road map shows how leadership shapes values, values drive culture, culture fosters teamwork, and this ecosystem ultimately drives performance. The idea of creating an enthusiastic environment where there is high performance and high fulfillment really inspires a talented workforce to do their best work. *More Than a Company* is a must read for anyone wanting to learn the recipe for long-term leadership success!

—**Jason Young,** *Former Leadership Development and Customer Service Trainer, Southwest Airlines; Founder, LeadSmart, Inc., and Culturetopia, LLC; Author,* The Culturetopia Effect *and* Servicetopia

The subtitle of Ron Scheese's book, *Leading in a Values-Based Ecosystem*, makes a bold claim, and this book does not let the reader down. Through sharing his own journey as a leader, Ron engages the reader in understanding the importance of actively developing a company's ecosystem around values, focusing on people rather than profit. This approach creates as much, if not more, value for the company than a profit-based approach. A must-read book for anyone in a leadership role or aspiring to such a role, either in the for-profit or not-for-profit world.

—Jacquelyn S. Fetrow, *President and Professor of Chemistry and Biochemistry, Albright College*

Ron Scheese masterfully sets the stage for values-based leadership in any organization, and specifically in employee-owned companies. Ron developed his framework at the forefront of the business as a CEO. It's real, engaging, and transformative. You feel like a fly on the wall watching over the shoulders how Ron leads his team and the whole organization.

—Dave Osh, *CEO, Varlinx*

Ron Scheese is the kind of leader who knows the difference between employee engagement and employee satisfaction and understands why the first is more important than the second. Read this book, and you'll see how he was able to diagnose a critical problem Andesa faced in 2016 and launch a program that re-energized the entire company, leading to sharp increases in revenue, income, employee retention, and assessed value. We need more leaders like him.

—Bo Burlingham, *Author* Small Giants; *Coauthor,* The Great Game of Business

Ron Scheese's notion of an ecosystem reflects how the Alliance and its fraternal benefit societies unite for the greater good. *More Than a Company* is a helpful reminder that sharing values among your business partners is important.

—Allison Koppel, *CAE, Chief Executive Officer, American Fraternal Alliance*

more than
a company

RON SCHEESE

more than
a company

leading in a
VALUES-BASED
ecosystem

Published by Advantage, Charleston, South Carolina.
Member of Advantage Media Group.

ADVANTAGE is a registered trademark, and the Advantage colophon is a trademark of Advantage Media Group, Inc.

Printed in the United States of America.

10 9 8 7 6 5 4 3 2 1

ISBN: 978-1-64225-302-3
LCCN: 2021905995

Cover design by Megan Elger.
Layout design by Mary Hamilton.

This publication is designed to provide accurate and authoritative information in regard to the subject matter covered. It is sold with the understanding that the publisher is not engaged in rendering legal, accounting, or other professional services. If legal advice or other expert assistance is required, the services of a competent professional person should be sought.

 Advantage Media Group is proud to be a part of the Tree Neutral® program. Tree Neutral offsets the number of trees consumed in the production and printing of this book by taking proactive steps such as planting trees in direct proportion to the number of trees used to print books. To learn more about Tree Neutral, please visit **www.treeneutral.com**.

Advantage Media Group is a publisher of business, self-improvement, and professional development books and online learning. We help entrepreneurs, business leaders, and professionals share their Stories, Passion, and Knowledge to help others Learn & Grow. Do you have a manuscript or book idea that you would like us to consider for publishing? Please visit **advantagefamily.com**.

To those who paved the road before me, shared the journey with me, and will carry on the Andesa Forever quest.

My life is RICHIR because of you.

CONTENTS

INTRODUCTION

The unexamined life is not worth living.
—Socrates

I am a lifelong learner. Learning doesn't end when we leave the classroom and walk across a graduation stage. If you picked up this book on the importance of values to business culture, I believe we have something in common: an innate desire to learn. We all experience many lessons along life's journey, and my latest have come during my service as CEO of Andesa Services.

I value education because it was my ticket out of poverty. I was the middle child born to loving, supportive, and encouraging parents in the Coal Region of Eastern Pennsylvania. My father was a World War II sergeant who provided for us by driving a tractor trailer and laboring for Bethlehem Steel mining. His best encouragement was to "study hard and get a job where you use your brain." He appreciated the value of hard work, but he hoped his children wouldn't struggle as he'd toiled just to scratch out a living. My mom was a homemaker raising five children. Her spark was a sense of humor and a spirit of generosity, service, and giving.

When you have little, you have each other. While I couldn't comprehend how poor we were, I knew my parents expected more from us and wanted more for us. Faith, love, humor, and high expectations for performance in athletics and in the classroom defined the environment my parents created to ensure my brothers and sisters and I could live a more meaningful life.

The importance of education was reinforced by several beloved teachers and coaches. When I majored in accounting at Albright College in Reading, Pennsylvania, many professors challenged me to contemplate situations through a myriad of perspectives. My Albright friends' parents owned businesses or were executives in large companies. In addition to the classroom setting, through countless casual conversations with those friends, I experienced a world different than that of Coaldale, Pennsylvania. Decades later, I am honored to serve my alma mater as chair of the board of trustees to help ensure future generations will experience the profound positive impact of a liberal arts education.

My career as a certified public accountant began at Ernst & Young as a financial auditor. In many ways, public accounting furthered my business education. I was a sponge, absorbing all I could while being exposed to clients in multiple industries and facing various financial challenges.

A series of career moves over the next decades resulted in multiple financial leadership roles for several faith-based healthcare organizations and technology companies. I developed a five- to seven-year cyclical pattern of career changes. At about that mark, I sensed I had made a positive impact on the organization, but I felt myself becoming stagnant, not learning, and unchallenged. I was feeling this way in 2005 when I first learned about Andesa Services.

When one becomes associated with Andesa, it doesn't take long to recognize its unique culture. From my initial encounter with Andesa's founder, John Walker, I understood this would be a man from whom I would learn and grow. He radiated a strong presence and a deep sense of purpose. John created something much more special than a profitable company. He created a vision of a purpose-driven, ethical environment that moves humanity forward through advancement of its people and clients. In his book *Value from Values: The Making of Andesa Services*, John describes the secret sauce of Andesa's unique culture: "To say that a firm has a soul is to say that it has incorporated into its operating procedures strong ethical values and an uncompromising concern for the welfare of its employees."[1]

Through a variety of experiences and seasons over the course of my career, I had developed strong financial, analytical, risk-management, leadership, business, and strategic planning skills. I quickly understood that in assuming the CEO role at Andesa, I had responsibility for the environment in which our employees spent a large portion of their time and earned their livelihoods for their families. That seemingly simple shift in logic was the key to becoming a leader in a people-first versus profit-first environment. As a CPA, I dream in numbers, so it was a challenge to change my mindset and learn to make our culture and environment my focus. As with most lessons, this one took years to learn and a few hard knocks along the journey.

This is not a philosophical or an academic book. The chapters ahead provide real-life examples of values-based leadership applied in the setting of a specific unique culture, an environment grounded in an ethical culture, which encourages and facilitates its employee-

---

1   John Walker, *Value from Values: The Making of Andesa Services.*

owners to develop and apply their business skills to the fullest, for both clients and employee-owners to achieve their full potentials. Andesa's values would not necessarily align with the business model for every company; there is no "one size fits all" when it comes to values. But my hope is that our example provides lessons to be learned regarding the importance of values, getting them right, and getting the alignment necessary to sustain a high-performing culture and drive operational performance across an ecosystem of suppliers and clients.

I sometimes get criticized for being naïve or having a rose-colored view of the world. Does this whole values-based, people-first culture thing really work? Does it translate into business success?

Andesa has had a thirty-five-plus-year track record of growth and reinvention by adhering to this approach. After a disappointing employee-engagement survey score in 2016, we stressed the examination and integration of our values efforts in the employee environment. Since then, our revenues are up 20 percent, our net income is up 27 percent, our employee retention improved from around 80 percent annually to above 90 percent, and company value as measured by an independent valuation firm for employee stock ownership plan purposes has increased by more than 60 percent. While I would like to have a longer track record of those performance measures, the simple fact is that the company has had a different trajectory since we embraced this approach. We continue to invest in the company and in the values-based, people-first model, and we are not done yet.

Today I am blessed to lead this company where my purpose, passion, spirit, and work align—one which, in many ways, echoes the values and experiences I learned from my parents, teachers, and so many friends and mentors over my thirty-five-plus-year career. As you journey through the Andesa stories and values, I hope you begin to appreciate how important a values-based leadership approach is to building and sustaining culture. If I can encourage you to understand, reflect, and adopt values-based leadership early in your career, it's my belief that you, your organization, and the world will be the better for it. I truly hope you are encouraged to find your purpose and work toward it, to put more into the world than you expect to take from it.

Let's dig deeper into my Andesa journey.

CHAPTER ONE

Values—An Individual Understanding

If the people aren't looking out for the community, then the benefits of a community erode. Many companies have star employees, but few have a culture that produces great people as a rule and not an exception.
—Simon Sinek, *Start with Why*

"It seems you change jobs every five to seven years," Linda Ellison observed during one of my initial interviews at Andesa. "What would make us believe you'd stay at Andesa?"

"I don't think I will," I replied. "I think I'll learn a little, help make the company stronger, and then will probably be looking for my next challenge in five to seven years. I looked at your financials. I know they can be improved. It will take some time, but I do know that when I leave, Andesa's financial position will be in better shape than it is now." Looking back on it now, I cringe recalling that response, which must have come across as more than a bit arrogant—but at least it was honest.

In a subsequent interview, this time with Andesa's founder and board chair, I was asked, "Have you read Tom Friedman's *The World Is Flat*? I think there are some similarities with Andesa. How do you see it?" I had read the book, and that precipitated a terrific, wide-ranging conversation about the importance of education, empowering individuals, technology, and collaboration with John, both of us sharing our career and life experiences.

What I did not realize as I passed through the hiring process was that Andesa was actually interviewing me for my values, looking for insights into what made me tick and how I might respond to the difficult challenges one often faces in business. Certainly, I gave them little or no reason to think that I understood the importance of the alignment of personal and corporate values in the workplace—but they took a chance that I would grow into an understanding and appreciation for their culture and decide to stay.

Little did I know then that the "next challenge" I'd envisioned as being five to seven years in my future would actually come at Andesa—the opportunity to lead the company as the CEO. With some tenure in that role, I can tell you the experience has been a learning laboratory. With new challenges coming at us regularly, I've often needed to rely on the hard-won wisdom garnered through the experiences I've navigated over my career. However, there are also days where those new challenges and situations present opportunities I never imagined. Perhaps my biggest lesson has been growing to better understand and appreciate the importance of culture and values.

We talk a lot about values at Andesa. That's only natural; values are intrinsic to what we do for our clients. We provide the tools and data that assist them, their sales teams, and those covered by the insurance in the management of these life insurance policies. In a highly complex insurance marketplace that demands accurate policy values, Andesa has enjoyed a successful thirty-five-plus-year track record because it provides *correct* values on our clients' policies.

Andesa's team also talks a lot about the other kind of values—those we expect our employee-owners to personify in all they do: **respect, integrity, courage, honesty, initiative, and responsibility**—our **RICHIR** values. You'll learn more about these in subsequent chapters, but it's my belief that Andesa has enjoyed that successful thirty-five-plus-year track record because it embraces these values as well.

Where Our Values Come From (and Why It Matters)

Learning and new experiences have always been motivators for me. It has been my good fortune to have great opportunities and excellent mentors along the way. Early in my career, when the job change "itch" hit, it was either because the learning opportunities in my current position had dried up or because I could see I had a chance to learn more in another role. When I initially interviewed at Andesa, I saw it as just another occasion to demonstrate my skills and experience.

Then I met John Walker.

Andesa's founder is all heart and soul. His moral compass is the underlying "why" behind the success of Andesa. John believes in the intrinsic worth of each individual and the power of the human spirit. My own personal growth and transformation from a number-crunching, results-oriented executive to a values-based, culture-first leader has come through countless conversations with John in which I was both challenged and encouraged.

In his book *Good Profit*, Charles Koch notes that "every organization has its own culture. If that culture is not created consciously and purposively, it will degenerate into a cult of personality or an 'anything goes' environment."[2] For Andesa to perpetuate the founder's values, the organization must emphasize a process by which it hires for values. Through many Andesa stories and conversations with John over the years, it became apparent to me that hiring for values and *then* teaching skills is a critical component in maintaining that critical moral compass through the ups and downs of economic cycles and the challenges presented by technological and societal changes. If one desires to build a company to last one hundred years—as we say, a Forever Vision—the organization will inevitably experience many changes. But its core character—what employees and clients can trust and expect—cannot deviate. Upholding those values is critical—and challenging.

> Hiring for values and then teaching skills is a critical component in maintaining that critical moral compass through the ups and downs.

When I think back on my career, I regret that it took me so long to see that the value of an individual is so much greater than just what they can contribute to the business. Their worth to the business pales in comparison to their value as a person—someone who deserves patience, love, and encouragement as they strive to reach their full potential. After all, that is what John did for me—he challenged me to think differently and pushed me to grow as a leader and a person. Recognizing earlier on that a culture that frees people to reach their

---

2   Charles G. Koch, *Good Profit: How Creating Value for Others Built One of the World's Most Successful Companies* (New York: Currency Books, 2015), 120.

full potential leads to business success would have made my career much more rewarding, meaningful, and impactful. That is one of the most valuable lessons I've learned at Andesa and in moving from CFO to CEO responsibilities.

A company's CEO needs to be the heart and soul of the business. Tasked with being the core keeper of the culture and DNA, a leader must also be able to enlist the energy of a whole cadre of people to buy into it. It recently warmed my heart when a manager shared, "You know that 'full potential' thing you talk about means more than just their role or their job? It's about their whole life." I smiled because it was a reminder that we continue to build the institutional muscle necessary to perpetuate the Andesa vision and culture. Perhaps the hundred-year goal is achievable, after all.

I don't think Andesa is unique in its approach. I do think the original values of most organizations stem from the personal values of their founder. The entrepreneur translates their personal beliefs and priorities into the spirit of the business—how the organization conducts its business. Over time, those personal values become the company's values—its soul, if you will.

Not all we do is correct, not every interaction or relationship is a good one, but our values are the driving force behind our efforts as we aspire to prove our founder's vision that there is a right way to conduct business. When you put your values out there, when you strive to live those values in everything you do, every interaction, every transaction, you attract people of strong moral fiber who wish to belong and contribute to that meaningful mission. Those who align closely with Andesa and our culture do so because they, too, believe in the worth of the individual and the power of the human spirit.

Not everyone shares those beliefs when they first come on board, of course. Some come to our organization prioritizing income and view the company solely through a transactional lens. Yet we see many grow personally and professionally through exposure to an ethical, values-based environment. Surrounded by values-based associates, these individuals engage with mentors, have conversations about values, reflect on their personal CliftonStrengths assessment, and take responsibility for challenging work. They act in accordance with the norms and expectations of the culture—and they thrive.

Andesa's employees learn their jobs, not in a classroom or training room setting, but primarily by observing others perform their own jobs and via hands-on opportunities. The relationships built in the learning process create the bonds of community and provide a natural opportunity to convey values and culture in such a way that no orientation or training video could. For those doing the training, sharing our culture with new employees enhances their own commitment to it, even as it preserves our vision and values.

Yes, even Andesa has its fair share of turnover—but our overall retention rate typically hovers around 90 percent. We have found that values have value at Andesa.

Learning to Do Better: An Ongoing Effort

All that said, we're still learning—and we learned a most powerful lesson in 2016. Our retention rate had slipped closer to 80 percent. We were about nine months into actualizing our new strategic plan, but clearly, something was off. The cost of recruitment was eating into our profitability. No sooner had we onboarded and trained new hires than we were recruiting for those roles again, or so it seemed. That was when we pivoted from our annual employee satisfaction survey to a survey that measured employee engagement.

Engagement and satisfaction are two totally different things. Employee engagement measures an employee's sense of connection to their work. Questions such as "Am I contributing and making an impact?" and "Do I care about my company and its success?" get to the heart of engagement. Satisfaction is more about job enjoyment— "Am I happy?" For example, an employee who feels overpaid, unchallenged, and watches videos all day when you think they are working hard may be very happy and satisfied with that situation. But they are certainly not engaged and contributing to the business. Engaged employees are satisfied employees but satisfied employees are not always engaged.

The results of the employee-engagement survey showed Andesa ranked in the thirty-sixth percentile, meaning 64 percent of all surveyed companies were doing a better job of engaging their employees. For a company that strived to be an employee-centric company with a stated purpose of helping employees reach their full potential, this was devastating news. It was a gut-check moment for me when I realized that rather than leading, I had settled for being the steward of John's company—acting more like a caretaker than a trailblazer.

Our response was twofold. First, we invested in leadership development. Second, we went back to our roots with a renewed focus on values and culture.

For leadership development, we partnered with the talented team at TAG Consulting. Several senior leaders received one-on-one leadership coaching, and a larger group met frequently for additional training on transformational leadership skills. We began to intervene on the environmental and engagement issues that had been flagged in our employee-engagement survey. These efforts bore fruit as we saw growth in the camaraderie, teamwork, and trust among the leadership team and resolved issues that mattered to the employees. The projects also demonstrated how all employee-owners could collaborate to improve the environment.

With leadership development well underway, we started work on our values and culture. While Andesa had always been a values-based, employee-centric company, we seemed to have lost sight of our roots. If we were going to improve the ways we interacted within the Andesa environment, it had to start with the people, their assumptions, and their beliefs.

We began a series of conversations about the company's values with about thirty nonmanagement employees. Three breakout groups of ten individuals were drawn from across the company. Composed mostly of volunteers, they were a good representation of our employee population, from the most tenured to those who'd recently joined us right out of college. Different genders, ethnicities, skill sets, educational backgrounds, and multiple faiths were represented.

We modeled our approach after a framework borrowed from one of my mentors, James Osterhaus, in his book *Gettysburg and Leadership*. Each value conversation session included a short, thought-provoking exercise to stimulate creative thinking about a given value and a series of consistent questions about each identified value: "What does this mean? Where do you see this value exhibited at Andesa? Where are you challenged to live this value in your work?" and so on.

Going into the conversations, I'd been worried that Andesa's values had become stale. Conventional wisdom says "traditional" values don't resonate with the younger generation; did our values have the marketing appeal necessary to attract top talent to a company whose predominant business was technology and the service behind that technology? I had fallen prey to the hype that moral decline was eating away at our country's fundamental character and our society no longer cherished humility, kindness, bravery, decency, integrity, loyalty, honesty, and other so-called eulogy virtues.

I assumed Andesa would emerge from this deep dive into its culture with new language and renewed energy to fuel our recommitment to our values. I didn't anticipate that new values would emerge—after all, we are who we are—but I did expect updated language and a fresher way of articulating these principles. I certainly expected something flashier and sexier than respect, integrity, courage, honesty, initiative, and responsibility to emerge. But as the employees experienced their own self-awareness and wrestled with the concepts and values in their lives and in their company, three critical truths became clear.

The first of these was how profoundly our understanding of the values was deepened simply by examining them through these very different points of view. Each employee brought their unique understandings to their individual definitions of each value. Yes, the words resonated for all of them—but their meanings were shaded by their life and work experiences, so everyone experienced them differently.

The second critical lesson was a significant "aha" moment. We realized our values—respect, integrity, courage, honesty, initiative, and responsibility—weren't the company's values at all. These were the core values of the individuals that came to work with us. The environment allowed each employee to be themselves and act in accordance with their values. It affected the way team members interacted with one another and with our clients. The result was that the employees' personal values became the company's values. While this is often the case with a founder's value set becoming the company's value set, by hiring for values, Andesa had been able to perpetuate a circular process by which the values of the individuals attracted to Andesa because of the values become the behaviors that define the company's values.

Remember my own Andesa recruitment story—how John and Linda were interviewing me for values, but I didn't appreciate or understand that at the time? The conversations with our employees made this crystal clear to me: Each person who joins the organization can build and sustain the culture or slowly erode it over time. If we were going to preserve the integrity of our culture, we collectively needed to go to the heart of the recruitment process and make the best possible hiring decisions.

When the groups examined occasions in which Andesa's employees had exemplified the values, particularly in situations where it was challenging to live the values or where values competed with one another, it was clear that each of these decision points created an opportunity to contribute to the culture or detract from it. We all gained an appreciation for the commitment necessary to build and sustain a vibrant, values-based culture. Examination of these situations also showed that the interpretation of the values was through the lens of the recipient of the encounter, not the provider of the service. For example, if I believe I am communicating honestly but the recipient has a different interpretation and expectation of honesty, the relationship can be eroded. If more and more employees "bend the edges" of a value to achieve personal gain versus the corporate good, "ethical fading" slowly erodes the culture.

Creating Cultural Champions

To counteract ethical fading, the organization needs constant attention to and reminders of the expected behaviors the corporate values are intended to produce. At Andesa, the values conversations resulted in the development of several employees into what we call "culture champions." Each of them took one of the values and presented the group's findings to the leadership team. They then collaborated on a booklet, titled *Andesa Forever*, which was sort of a code of conduct for onboarding new employees. The booklet provides insights into Andesa's vision and definitions for each of our values, including examples of challenging situations and appropriate behaviors expected of Andesa employees.

Through the values focus groups and leadership development efforts, changes were happening for me as well. My leadership style shifted from a numbers-first, results-based approach to one focused on values and culture. In many ways, my personal leadership responsibilities became much more aligned with my personal vision, values, and purpose.

Let me share a few employee stories to demonstrate what it means to live Andesa's RICHIR values and to be employed at an employee-centric company.

- Jen Sell, Kim Matlack, Tammy Staudt, and Jessica Gauthier all began their Andesa journey in the office administrator role with receptionist responsibilities and executive assistant duties. Encouraged by a supportive environment, each pursued additional training and transitioned to new roles of finance and contracting paralegal, human resources administrator, marketing coordinator, and talent acquisition coordinator, respectively. Through work on various employee committees at Andesa, they have taken on roles that have a tremendous influence on the culture and spirit of the company.

- Bob Schoenberger came to Andesa in the winter of 2015 in the role of manager of IT operations, responsible for all data center operations, servers, storage, network, security, and telephony infrastructure, joining Andesa at a time when overall technology leadership was in transition. From our values-based recruiting process, we knew Bob was up to the challenge. He was asked to study the technology plans that had been developed previously and recommend a strategy for strengthening the technology footprint, with emphasis on growth and scalability. Bob and his team came forward with a recommendation for a three-year system overhaul project. Entrusted with the authority and autonomy to execute, Bob built a team of talented technologists capable of the implementation. The team delivered on the commitment, completing the project ahead of schedule and under budget. Bob and his team continue to keep the Andesa core systems state of the art through a cost-effective, disciplined, and evergreen process he proposed as part of the initial recommendation.

- Ryan Scanlan joined Andesa in 2019 as an IT security auditor. In less than a year with the firm, Ryan obtained a key industry certification for the work he does. Ryan and I worked together on our new-hire mentoring program and enjoyed numerous conversations about business and life. One of Ryan's assignments was to study where he saw the Andesa values being lived in the day-to-day work and report back. His analysis was deep and meaningful. He was then asked to write his findings into a blog post for our company's website, where his *Values in Action—an Employee's Viewpoint* was published in the summer of 2019. More recently, Ryan became a key part of the Andesa Pandemic Response Team. That team recommended ways to keep our employees safe and our operations efficiently functioning to support our clients during the COVID-19 pandemic. His influence and leadership abilities continue to grow.

The achievement of our full potential is a lifelong journey, not a destination. We measure progress by how far we've come, not against some ideal of potential realized. Being better tomorrow or next year is how we measure success. For many, that occurs within the Andesa environment and the company is better for it.

> The achievement of our full potential is a lifelong journey, not a destination.

At its core, an employee-centric environment starts with respect for the individual and the values-based relationship they establish with their team. Everyone is at a different point in their professional journey when they come to Andesa. A leader must take the time to understand an individual's strengths and aspirations, then match those to the company's needs. For some, that means entry-level business mentoring and opportunities to learn the business. Some are afforded the creativity and whiteboard-type challenges to be influencers or to take on a leadership role, whereas others are more motivated by being an individual contributor. That choice is equally valuable to the company, respected, and acceptable.

All employees bring their talents and gifts to the organization. It is the leader's responsibility to help the individuals flourish and create an environment where they can thrive and make a difference. Since each employee is at a different stage in their personal journey, situational leadership is essential. Sometimes additional training or coaching is needed. Other times, a strong challenge may be necessary, or a mentor-type support structure is helpful. Far from being one-sided, the mentor/mentee relationship is one that rewards both participants with inspiration and personal growth.

And Our Clients Are Paying Attention Too

The third critical lesson was that customers and clients evaluate the organization through a values lens as well. While the values alignment of individuals who work for the organization is necessary to sustain the culture, alignment with a company's customers and clients is equally important.

The initial encounter with a client may be prompted by a specific problem they have that needs a solution or may simply be transactional in nature. But over time, a long-standing relationship develops because the provider of the product or service is delivering an experience valued by the recipient. While economics certainly weighs heavily in that relationship, when there is also values congruence, the resulting relationship can be blessed with both trust and longevity.

Andesa's clients are primarily life and annuity insurance entities. We strive to maintain a true partnership with each client. Because of the importance of the systems and services we provide, our team is truly an extension of our clients' operating departments. In addition to helping our employees reach their full potential, Andesa's vision places the same expectation on our client relationships—helping them achieve their full potential, as well. For the employee-client-organization relationship to be successful and endure through generations, it is imperative that our organizations share common core values and operate in accordance with them.

The life insurance industry is a noble industry. Life insurance can protect a family in the event of the death of a key bread winner or provide a way to transfer assets to family members or charitable institutions, or fund benefits and facilitate owner succession in a business setting. Life insurance is a promise by an entity of a payment in the future at one of the most difficult moments in the life cycle of a business or family. It is a contract of utmost good faith by both parties. Consider the challenges an insurance company must navigate as it sells a policy to a twenty-year-old, guaranteeing a long-term product that often assumes that a claim settlement may not be necessary for possibly sixty or seventy years. The insurance company must bear the risk of economic, societal, and regulatory change as well as medical advances, technological changes, etc. to meet the purchaser's need for financial security far into the future. It is long term, and it is values based. We may live in an instant-gratification society, but when it comes to entrusting a company with my family's or business's well-being in my absence, I admire an industry that will endure and be there when I need it most.

We could easily compare Andesa's culture and values with the values language expressed on the websites of a few of our clients:

COMPANY	VALUES
Cigna	• We care deeply about our customers, patients, and coworkers • We create a better future—together • We innovate and adapt • We partner, collaborate, and keep our promises • We act with speed and purpose
Equitable	• We have a passion for our business • We work to the highest standards • We are a trusted partner to our clients • We treat everyone with respect and dignity • We are stronger as a team

COMPANY	VALUES
Lincoln Financial	• Integrity • Respect • Responsibility
New York Life	• Integrity • Reliability • Humanity
Protective	• Do the right thing • Serve people • Build trust • Simplify everything
Symetra Financial	• Value • Transparency • Sustainability

The old adage "People like doing business with people they like" is a statement that gets to the heart of relationships in business. Andesa's journey provides evidence that if you can align your personal values with that of your company, the vendors and partners with which you do business, and the clients and customers you serve, you have an opportunity to create a powerful ecosystem that will result in a successful, enduring business.

How does this values congruence operate on a day-to-day basis and translate into long-term business success? Let's examine Andesa's ecosystem in the next chapter.

CHAPTER TWO
Building an Ecosystem

The greatest and most inspiring mountain climbing
achievements in history are not so much stories of individual
achievement but are stories of the extraordinary power of a
unified, talented, prepared team that stays loyally committed
to one another and to their shared vision to the end.
—**Stephen Covey,** *The 8th Habit*

"Our team was impressed with your team today. It is clear to us why so many top-tier companies are aligned with you," the vice president of marketing of a large insurance company told me. Our teams had spent an entire day on a deep-dive session to understand this prospect's plans and needs as well as educate them on Andesa's systems and capabilities. I had joined the group for a postmeeting dinner. "Probably more important is how our cultures and values align," he continued. "The reason we want to do business with you is your values. And we will be doing business together."

Seven months later we were ready to begin our first project with this client. It was a relatively small project for us, but it came with a condensed time frame. The solution had to be ready in time to enroll a large new life insurance case—but it was caught up in the legal and procurement bureaucracy common to large companies. We did not have defined requirements from the client nor a signed contract. With a looming deadline on the horizon, our team evaluated the situation and decided, "Let's get started. This could lead to a larger and longer lasting client partnership. This is just step one. If we work on this project for the next four months and the client backs out, we have some financial exposure, but it's worth the risk." Everything about our courage, responsibility, and initiative values said, "Let's go." About a third of the way through the project, the contract still was not signed. It was time for a gut check. The Andesa team met with the client team members to present a demo of what we had built so far. The reviews were excellent, and the client spokesperson said, "This is why we chose you." The signed statement of work came through shortly afterward, and we legally commenced a new relationship, one that began many months earlier, and one I'm confident will be long-term and mutually beneficial.

Could Andesa have lost money on that project? Yes! Would we risk that on every project? No. Business is about the assessment of risk—but in our world, business is viewed through our prism of values. While personal and corporate-level thinking is critical to business success, it is also important to align one's personal and business values with a larger, more global perspective as well. A leader must also have the perspective of the role of the business within a larger ecosystem of suppliers, customers, community, and society.

The Andesa Ecosystem

Scientifically speaking, an ecosystem is a community of living organisms interacting as a system in conjunction with the nonliving components of their environment. These components are linked together through nutrient cycles and energy flows. In general, business or technology professionals use the term "ecosystem" to define a complex network of interconnected systems. A business ecosystem is a living system that must adapt to a changing environment. Within an ecosystem, each participant contributes to and benefits from the system's ability to adapt and change.

> Within an ecosystem, each participant contributes to and benefits from the system's ability to adapt and change.

Does every business have an ecosystem? As I reflect on my experiences—the interplay between professors, staff, alumni, students, and community in a higher education organization or the physicians, nurses, administration, staff, patients, and community that interact in a healthcare system; or the employees, vendors and clients in a business environment—the answer is clearly yes. A more important question is, "Will you, as the leader, create the environment you want, or will it be created for you?" A business can purposefully build and nurture its ecosystem, or that ecosystem can be left to form on its own. To intentionally build an ecosystem for your business, you've got to begin with a foundation of vision and values.

The word *ecosystem* used to describe the relationship between Andesa's employees, environment, clients, and systems was born of a long and heated discussion with my colleagues at the start of our new strategic planning cycle in 2015. What was our deep "Why?"—our core focus, our core passion? We all had our own ideas about that, but as we debated, we realized that we kept coming back to the same place: the primacy of relationships to everything we are. Rich relationships—whether between team members or with clients—are our driving force and the place from which we derive our energy.

Through those discussions, we developed a clear and focused understanding of our core ideology—the understanding of the Andesa ecosystem. We focused on how to nurture these critical relationships: building our teams, encouraging each other, and forging partnerships with our clients, all of which would build our business over the long term.

Many business books offer advice on how to build a business, lead a department, or manage a team—but I'd like to encourage taking a broader view. Thinking about your company, departmental, or team responsibilities as an ecosystem consisting of relationships offers a powerful perspective. Unless you purposefully craft the ecosystem, the environment may be completely alien to your values, and your business may bear no resemblance to your stated vision or purpose. Earlier, we discussed the importance of hiring for values since each person hired has the potential to either build the culture or cause the culture to fade. Likewise, every business decision places a different pressure on the business. Be very intentional about purpose and the preservation of the values of the ecosystem as you embark on these changes and grow.

Building a Vibrant Ecosystem

Stephen Covey's eighth habit is to "find your voice and inspire others to find theirs." The message "find your voice" points out the critical need for self-reflection and self-awareness. Know what is important to you! "Inspire others to find theirs" is an honorable call to serve others, to help build up others to achieve their potential. To build a strong, sustainable ecosystem, begin by developing your people. Good people make for good products, good services, good businesses, good relationships and good ecosystems.

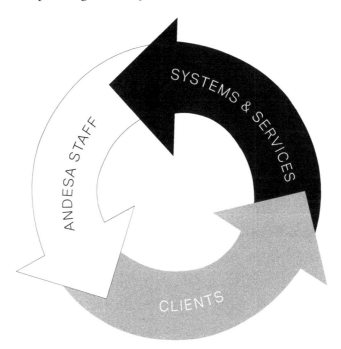

Andesa's "voice" is an ecosystem that constantly encourages the development of special relationships between systems, services, staff, and clients. It is an environment in which each person contributes to the ecosystem and is supported and encouraged to reach their full potential. As each component grows stronger, they strengthen the system through their individual contributions and efforts.

Our focus on relationships allows Andesa to offer its clients a unique combination of people, ideas, technology, and trust. It has helped Andesa and our clients to successfully navigate periods of regulatory change, technological advancement, environmental upheaval, security risks, and the ups and downs of business cycles. The ecosystem is successful because its foundation is built upon values and relationships that align leadership, employees, and clients.

The ecosystem makes for a stronger Andesa, which means it can make greater investments in people and technology—and our clients reap the benefits. As an example, from a technology perspective, Andesa tends to cocreate systems. This means rather than building small applications to supplement our large processing systems and selling them to our clients, we often partner with a single client. A client may approach us with a problem or an idea and ask, "Can your system do this?" Sometimes the answer is, "No, but we can create it, and we can partner with you to build it." Approximately 90 percent of the time, we are not doing unique or proprietary work for the client, so we eventually add the new functionality to our base system. In the meantime, the initial client has the advantage of being first in the market with the new functionality and gets the opportunity to design the requirements specific to their needs. As we build more modules, more tools, and more ways to analyze information, those changes become available to our other clients as part of the overall system. The entire ecosystem benefits.

James L. Heskett, W. Earl Sasser, and Leonard Schlesinger captured this concept in an article in the *Harvard Business Review* in 1994.[3] They called it the **service-profit chain**. The service-profit chain links employee satisfaction to customer loyalty and ultimately to financial results in a sustainable ecosystem. John Walker built the model over a decade earlier at Andesa, purposefully constructing an ethical environment that strives to improve the lives of our values-

---

3   James L. Heskett et al., "Putting the Service-Profit Chain to Work," *Harvard Business Review* 72, no. 2 (March–April 1994): 164–174.

based employees, who in turn invest their energy to improve the experience and results for our clients, which leads to client loyalty and long-term system and organizational stability and success.

The system works because the components are tethered by relationships—and because of the alignment of values between business and client. If the purpose of Andesa was just to get big so that we could exit to the highest bidder, that would be an anathema to our clients. Their business model necessitates a vision for the long term. Their policyholders expect it; how could they put their trust in a company that is short-term focused? With our values and Forever Vision approach, Andesa's clients understand who will be backing the software-as-a-service model promise decades from now.

Andesa can realize its potential and accomplish its goals by helping its clients accomplish their goals—by finding our voice and helping others find their voice too. It is not a typical vendor-client relationship we seek to build; it is a true partnership in which we become an extension of our client's operations, plans, aspirations, and results. When this partnership is achieved, the whole ecosystem is strengthened.

Means, Ends, and the Real Measure of Success

What would you do to succeed? One of our founder's core beliefs and one we espouse at Andesa Services is that "the ends never justify the means. All we do indelibly imprints our final product."

Too often, the "win at all costs" philosophy and achievement-driven society motivates people to wink at inappropriate or marginal means as acceptable behavior. At Andesa, we would rather be measured and recognized for how we conduct ourselves, instead of solely on the results we achieve. Like it or not, we are all judged by our results (ends). With the employees as the focus of our work ("the ends") and the adoption of a belief statement like "the ends never justify the means," we guard against marginal behavior or short-term, results-oriented thinking. This helps preserve the ecosystem for the long haul. Good means feed an ecosystem; bad means can destroy one.

The prospect story at the beginning of this chapter is a good example of this concept. Did anyone on the team know that a signed contract was guaranteed? No. Could we have plowed money into that opportunity and suffered a financial loss? Yes. However, when the team assessed why we exist, what our purpose is, what our values say, what this short-term risk could mean for the long-term health of the ecosystem—the choice to proceed seemed natural. I'm sure we'll be faced with similar challenges in the future—and I trust we will make the values-based decision to do that which strengthens our ecosystem. If we think it is the right thing to do, we're going to do it, rather than being driven by an economic result, especially a short-term economic result.

Before I understood these concepts of ends and means, core values, and the importance of culture in the development of an ecosystem for a business, I had conversations with more than one employee where I said things like, "My job isn't to make you happy. My job is to get results." Today it's more like, "My job is to take care of the culture. My job is to figure out how to create an environment where employees want to come, give their best, and feel proud of their work. How can I help you do that?"

Empowering Employees Through Ownership

The transition of Andesa to 100 percent employee ownership via an employee stock ownership plan (ESOP) transaction by the founder and other shareholders is another example of what it means to empower the individual, which in turn builds the ecosystem. An ESOP is a qualified retirement benefit plan, similar to a 401(k), whereby the largest holding in the plan is often company stock, even if that company is privately held. The stock is held in a trust and the employees benefit over time from the returns of the company and brand they help grow and sustain.

This ESOP represents the final link in the service-profit chain noted earlier. Employee-owners take care of the environment, which leads to satisfied employees, who serve to satisfy the clients, which leads to long-term business success. The ESOP rewards the employee-owners who take care of the brand, environment, and clients in this ecosystem.

The ESOP transaction indicated to our clients that Andesa is serious about partnering for the long term. In a time when it is the norm for technology companies to have exit-focused mindsets, an ecosystem mindset is long-term and self-sustaining. Like our client partners who assume the risk, Andesa understands that when a client signs on with Andesa, we assume an obligation to support the technology that administers the life policies during the long life cycle of the underlying insured—a time frame often beyond the career tenure of the leadership making the commitment. The ESOP is a declaration of intent to remain private and support our ecosystem in collaboration and in congruence with the long-term vision and values of our client partners.

The ESOP is the vehicle through which Andesa can perpetuate its culture and ecosystem. Employee ownership is not the sole answer, but it is an economic piece that has the potential to build something to last for a hundred years. As employees think more like owners, they protect and advance the brand. This is *their* company; this is *their* culture. It is up to the collective group of individuals to keep it healthy and growing.

As an owner, part of every employee's job is to build the culture, to make sure the next generation is ready to assume the responsibilities, and to provide new employees with the support to be successful. An employee is not at Andesa just for their transaction ability. They are here to build something, create something, and own it. This is the ownership mentality of the ESOP. Each employee-owner benefits from helping their colleagues advance their careers because the overall ecosystem is made stronger. And at the end of the day, the ESOP is the ownership piece that now rewards the individual for being on this journey. Employee ownership is an investment in our belief of self-governance to allow for a long-term time horizon—a vision we call Andesa Forever. And the key element of that investment in our future is the personal growth of the employees who join Andesa.

When Andesa's employee-engagement scores were not where we expected in 2016, we didn't point fingers, lay blame, or terminate people. We invested in leadership as a first step. We saw it as an investment in our ecosystem. One of the outcomes of the investment in leadership development was a focus on training and personal development. We created a program called Andesa Academy. With appropriate guidance and tools, people are encouraged to take responsibility for their own learning and development. It was our aspiration that resources for self-development be made available to all members of the Andesa team. Andesa Academy gives our employees an avenue to discover and pursue their purpose, the autonomy to take the initiative to drive their own learning, and the opportunity to master the skills that are required in their jobs and for future progression. As part of that commitment, we also provided paid subscriptions for all staff to LinkedIn Learning. Personal growth is encouraged to provide long-term contributors to the ecosystem.

My personal growth as a values-based leader accelerated after the meetings with my employee colleagues about Andesa's RICHIR values. The process was cathartic for me. It became clear that a critical calling of a leader is to build and sustain a thriving ecosystem. We are so often focused on the to-do lists and the work immediately in front of us that we ignore that which gives life meaning. Because we strive to be more than a vendor to our clients, we can easily become so absorbed that we forget to sustain our ecosystem and maintain our culture. If we take care of ourselves first (individually) and, as an organization, take care of our employee-owners first, stronger colleague and client relationships will follow, and the system will produce results.

Become a CRABBY Leader

As you reflect on the possibility of building and sustaining a thriving ecosystem in your company versus a narrower definition of a business or an organization, I encourage you to be a CRABBY leader.

The CRABBY acronym emerged for me one day while on vacation at the beach. As I watched a beach-replenishment project executed by the Army Corps of Engineers, I was mesmerized by the process. Perhaps what most caught my eye was the towering, *Star Wars*–like, three-wheeled vehicle used by the managers to survey the beach and monitor project progress. In what seemed a flawless coordination of man and machine, the Coastal Research Amphibious Buggy, or "CRAB," was the perfect piece of equipment to allow the leaders to observe patterns and trends from a vantage point they would otherwise miss.

Like the beach, an ecosystem needs regular replenishment. So how do you do that? The acronym CRABBY can help you keep what's most important in mind:

C: *Clarity.* Take a clarity break. Leadership should be both active and reflective. As I watched the CRAB, it reminded me that I needed to schedule some quiet time in my calendar regularly. With too many meetings, the day-to-day chaos, and unplanned demands, some days it is difficult to see the big picture. A scheduled meeting with myself for some quality "think time" is a treasured part of my week. It is a great way to reduce the clutter and gain clarity on issues.

R: *Refrain.* Refrain from the details. Take time to analyze patterns, trends, systems and processes, not details. We tend to perceive what is happening in the moment without consideration to what led to that moment. Sometimes I find my intervention in a situation leads to a bigger problem if I haven't assessed the overall system and environment. By getting up on the CRAB and looking down at the whole environment, a better solution may be found that contributes to the overall progress of the environment.

A: *Advisors.* Surround yourself with trusted advisors. These individuals should have a strong sense of the organization's values and freely offer their opinions, even when they suspect those opinions won't be popular. These relationships should be based on mutual respect and not some quid-pro-quo expectation. My trusted connections often offer a fresh perspective that isn't visible from where I sit.

B: *Be transparent.* Be open and seek input from the individual(s) to whom you report. They will often have a different vantage point and potentially broader understanding. Tap into this knowledge network. Again, by sharing my honest views and soliciting perspectives and feedback, I find I am frequently exposed to other possibilities I haven't even considered.

B: *Back into the fray.* Get back on the ground. Climbing the CRAB for perspective is fine, but real impact requires active engagement. The supervising manager of the beach-replenishment project surveyed the beach from the CRAB but then returned to ground level to activate. Assessments are best done from on high, but results are achieved on the ground.

Y: *Yearn to learn.* Pursue learning as a passion. From my experience, the best leaders are constantly learning, networking, or reading to bring more knowledge to the table with each interaction. Learning opens me up to new ideas and challenges my biases and assumptions.

Like the view of a beach ecosystem replenishment project from the top of a CRAB, we can get a fresh perspective of organizational progress from a higher point of view. To make long-term, lasting impact, leaders need to spend some time looking down on the business and, yes, even be a little CRABBY from time to time.

In *Leadership on the Line*, authors Ron Heifetz and Marty Linsky say it another way: They introduce the idea that leaders

> To make long-term, lasting impact, leaders need to spend some time looking down on the business.

need to take themselves out of the day-to-day fray to understand what is truly going on. The metaphor they use is "getting off the dance floor" (operations) and "getting up on the balcony"—a phrase that has made its way into the Andesa Services lexicon. Often, just that simple change of viewpoint can bring clarity to patterns or connections that matter.

As we look out over the next ten years, Andesa's aim is to continue to strengthen its ecosystem. We plan to maintain and build those relationships that feed our ecosystem and eliminate those that don't. We intend to enhance our employee ownership culture, which contributes to strong client relationships and retention. We will strive to sustain an environment that honors our teammates as individuals. We're committed to engaging our clients through partnerships to advance their business goals. All of this will help us achieve a better, stronger ecosystem.

For the ecosystem to thrive, there needs to be alignment at the intersection of people, processes, and systems that connects the components of the ecosystem to the workings of the model. For Andesa, that begins with the alignment of our vision and values across employees, clients, and our systems and services.

Congruence requires a common language and clear expectations. One of the key discoveries from our group value discussions was that many individuals and organizations have varying interpretations of words like *respect, integrity, courage, honesty, initiative,* and *responsibility.* As we examined each word through the lens of Dr. Osterhaus's framework and discussed those key questions about definition, behaviors, measures, obstacles, etc., we strengthened our clarity and further enhanced our ecosystem.

We will examine each of Andesa's values in the next chapters to provide further insight into the culture-building process. I am also humbled and honored to share the personal reflections of friends from across the life insurance industry. These "Voices of the Industry" segments demonstrate the power when values align across the ecosystem.

CHAPTER THREE
Respect

*Without appreciation and respect for other people, true
leadership becomes ineffective, if not impossible.*
—George Foreman

It was the call no CEO ever wants to get—and the client certainly
didn't pull his punches. "I have to tell you that I'm feeling pretty
disappointed and let down by Andesa," their senior vice president for
the life insurance division told me bluntly. "You guys gotta fix this!"

We had a technology snafu on our hands. Our client had
converted to an Andesa system to provide insurance brokers better
information about their clients' policies. The solution we provided
had performed well in our test environments but, for several reasons,
did not work so well when implemented. Our client was frustrated.
Calls were coming in from angry brokers about reports that were
late or inaccurate. The client's staff was working extra hours into the

evenings and on weekends to babysit the system. It had been a rough month, and a resolution was not yet in sight.

No one likes to disappoint a colleague or client, especially when millions of dollars in investments are involved. This time, we had not only disappointed our client but, since our goal is to always meet or exceed our clients' expectations, we had let ourselves down as well.

Resolving the issues would call for a combination of hardware enhancements and software performance tuning. Both required time to implement. At the end of the next business cycle, an Andesa business analyst was on site at our client's location to monitor the client's experience firsthand and determine if there were further opportunities to improve the situation. All told, three monthly cycles elapsed before the problems were solved to everyone's satisfaction. In the end, and despite that rocky beginning, the respect that developed between the client team and the Andesa team during the initial implementation process was what salvaged the situation.

Respect does not mean an absence of conflict but instead recognizes that conflict, even intense conflict, is about an issue, not a person. Comments intended to cause personal harm or create some sort of power hierarchy rather than move toward problem resolution are not respectful. Healthy conflict can build mutual trust when individuals present issues and express feelings to collaborate toward problem resolution.

Our client had demonstrated tremendous respect for me and our company by being so forthcoming. The client's expectation for resolution wasn't harsh; it was straightforward and emotionally honest. The disappointment expressed by the client during the situation was reasonable given the circumstances but was unusual in the context of our historical relationship. Their expectations were grounded in respect; they understood we could resolve the issue. Because of the relationship that had been built over the years, Andesa was granted the opportunity to rectify the problem.

Imagine how that situation and phone call might have played out had we not had respect for one another. If our client had remained silent about the issue, a gap in our relationship would have developed and widened with each passing month. Absent that sense of respect, what was likely to follow was an erosion of trust, a weakened relationship, brand and reputation damage, a potentially lost client, and economic loss. With respect, our client continued to provide future opportunities to enhance our relationship and strengthen the overall ecosystem.

It Begins with Trust

Respect relies on a relationship built on the foundation of mutual trust. It is easy to invest in something or someone you deem worthy of your time or money—when you believe they deserve it. But it is something more profound to honor another person without expecting anything in return from the relationship. That is the cornerstone of living Andesa's value of respect. When respect is freely offered, the relationship is strengthened and the ecosystem flourishes. Mutual respect allows for both parties to build on that trust and move toward their full potential.

To live the value of respect, a person must first respect themselves. In his best-selling book *The Road to Character*, David Brooks proposes a profound definition of self-respect:

> *Self-respect is not the same as self-confidence or self-esteem. Self-respect is not based on IQ or any of the mental or physical gifts that help get you into a competitive college. It is not comparative. It is not earned by being better than other people*

at something. It is earned by being better than you used to be, by being dependable in times of testing, straight in times of temptation. It emerges in one who is morally dependable. Self-respect is produced by inner triumphs, not external ones. It can only be earned by a person who has endured some internal temptation, who has confronted their own weaknesses and who knows, "Well, if worse comes to worst, I can endure that. I can overcome that."[4]

Self-respect is the starting point for respecting others. It allows us to enter a relationship in which we can make positive deposits. The keys to establishing a healthy, trusting, and valued relationship are an honest and positive self-image and a humbled ego, which allows you to consider the other individual as worthy of respect. A mutual sense of value and worth is imperative in any relationship, be it peer to peer, employee and leader, mentor and mentee, or company and client.

Title-based respect derived from your position within the company and economic-based respect established via a transactional relationship such as employer-employee or customer-supplier are not the genuine personal level of respect I challenge you to consider. By simply being human, each person has dignity and is worthy of respect. Thus, every interaction with a colleague or with a client is an opportunity to extend respect, encouragement, and esteem to an individual; in other words, to make a deposit in the relationship.

> Every interaction with a colleague or with a client is an opportunity to extend respect, encouragement, and esteem to an individual.

---

4   David Brooks, *The Road to Character* (New York: Penguin Random House, 2015).

The use of a deposit analogy isn't meant to construe respect as a transactional investment with an expected return. When we at Andesa talk about respect, it's in terms of an action verb. It is in the action to give respect that we make deposits in the relationship. One of our employees described respect as a boomerang you must send out before it comes back to you. I like that analogy.

Each interaction can add to the relationship or detract from it, so a word of caution: We have all heard something along the lines of "it takes years to earn respect but only seconds to destroy it." Respect given represents small deposits that accumulate and grow over time. Disrespect is a one-time, large withdrawal. It is imperative that we appreciate this and strive to operate in a respectful manner in every encounter.

Case Study: When Toyota Lost Its Way

Toyota is an example of how quickly respect can evaporate. In 2010, Toyota suffered damage to its brand and reputation after the recall of more than six million vehicles due to sticky accelerator pads and floor mats. The technical snafu was not the damaging issue. What caused the negative attention and reputation impairment was the company did not operate in congruence with its historic core values.

The "Toyota Way" is the codified principles and values of Toyota Motor Corporation. "Continuous Quality Improvement" and "Respect for People" are its two main pillars. At its core, "Respect for People" entails the facilitation of personal growth and achievement for its employees to benefit them and all stakeholders in the Toyota ecosystem. I take that to mean it is necessary to develop good people in order to provide good products or good services.

Several principles of the Toyota Way focus on this element of human development. Leaders are expected to personally adopt the Toyota value system as well as embrace and promote the corporate philosophy. Employees are expected to collaborate, work in teams, and support one another, putting team success ahead of personal success. Finally, Toyota looks beyond its employees and seeks to challenge its business partners to do better and achieve more, essentially treating them as they treat their employees—a true measure of respect—building a stronger ecosystem in the process.

Given Toyota's much-touted emphasis on the value of respect, their sluggishness in the brake-pad recall response was jarringly out of character, certainly not in keeping with the Toyota Way—and their would-be customers looked elsewhere. It took many years for the company to recover from the reputational damage, not to mention the economic impacts of lost sales, a $1.2 billion Justice Department settlement and a $50 million National Highway Traffic Safety Administration fine.

Toyota's example reminds us respect can be easily lost when our actions appear to contradict our professed values. It also serves as a further lesson on the difficulty of living our values in challenging times. Yet those are precisely the moments when we must draw strength from our core values.

As our value focus groups took on the challenge of understanding respect as a value, an excerpt from John Walker's book *Value from Values* demanded a people-first, authentic approach to the concept:

> *In an ethical environment, the individual is respected. In order for management to succeed in guiding people toward good decision-making, the environment must have the well-being of its people at its core. Employees must trust their managers and coworkers to stand behind them. People must believe this respect*

to be honest respect, not a ruse aimed at manipulating them. For example, the employees of Andesa say they are motivated to work hard because they believe that the firm cares about them as whole people, not just as employees. They feel as though they mean something to the firm, and in turn, the firm means more than a paycheck to them. It is important to note that the creation of an insincerely caring environment designed solely to achieve greater productivity would reek of manipulation and would quickly lead to a loss of faith in the organization.[5]

Our values examination sessions started with a six-minute clip from the 2015 film *Steve Jobs*. In the video, Jobs and Steve Wozniak are arguing about recognizing the Apple II team members at the upcoming iMac product launch. Two gifted individuals with vastly different skill sets faced off in an intense public argument "about the people" versus "about the business." The conflict escalated to personal attacks, including accusations of lack of respect for each other. The scene ends with Woz exiting the theater with the parting shot, "It's not binary. You can be decent and gifted at the same time."[6] While the actual scene may never have happened and was written to produce a dramatic Hollywood effect, it served as an idea generator to begin the discussion about respect from different points of view and on different levels.

Our team came to understand that respect meant to value others ahead of self—to treat others the way you would expect to be treated. The word "treat" and its derivatives (treatment, treating, treated, etc.) dominated our conversations. Respect demands we recognize someone for their intrinsic value, see them as having great worth, and regard them fairly and with dignity, considerate of their

---

5   John Walker, *Value from Values: The Making of Andesa Services.*

6   *Steve Jobs*, directed by Danny Boyle (2015).

perspectives in all our interactions. The discussion stressed action toward each other in a way that honors the intrinsic value in each human and in a manner we expect or desire to be treated. Simply put, our goal is to arrive at work with our dignity and leave with our dignity intact, each day!

Charles G. Koch in *Good Profit: How Creating Value for Others Built One of the World's Most Successful Companies* explains the importance of this cultural dynamic in terms of sustaining a knowledge-based, employee-owned company like Andesa:

> *When a workplace culture of respect and trust is promoted, employees share their ideas and seek out the best knowledge to anticipate and solve problems. Verbal exchanges lead to the discovery of new and better ways to create value. When such exchanges are hampered by overbearing taboos, bureaucracy, systems, procedures, tenure, knowledge hoarding, egos, or hierarchy, knowledge sharing is stifled.[7]*

At Andesa, we focus on the employees as the "ends" of the organization (i.e., the purpose of the organization) rather than the "means" or resources of the organization. We strive to esteem each individual and tap into this value of respect as a source of energy. To be respected at work is to be treated fairly, heard, trusted, and acknowledged as a contributor. We all have an intrinsic need to be respected, to "leave with our dignity intact." My teammate Stephanie Corby shared her perception (and responsibility) as a project manager in this regard with her values focus group:

> *It is critical to project success that I fully respect each team member's role, ability, and capacity to meet project goals. Notice I did not say deadlines. When team members feel their opinion*

---

7   Koch, *Good Profit*, 167.

is respected, they naturally put more effort into the work that is valued, and they feel is accomplishing something—it's just human nature. Additionally, when people are goal-driven and not deadline-driven (usually a good balance of the two works best), they feel they have the freedom to put their best efforts forward and dig deep to do so. While this freedom is not always an option in the "real world," it is imperative to incorporate it for the sake of people feeling like they are productive, respected humans and not just "resources."

The team dynamic is important in how respect manifests itself at Andesa. Most individuals participate in multifunction teams, not just department organizational groupings. It could be a client project implementation team, client service team, internal project team, or a cross-departmental corporate organization initiative task force. This culture of participation results in engaged employees rather than spectators. Teams are empowered to engage the employee-owners and handle all matters within their authority with little management interference or intervention. Stephanie's words remind us that the kind of team-based approach necessary to sustain a knowledge-based ecosystem cannot survive or succeed unless each member has confidence and respect in their teammates.

Respect in Action

I first met entrepreneur Chris Murumets a few years after after he had cofounded LOGiQ³, a technology company serving the life reinsurance industry. I asked Chris to share his reflections on the importance of respect in his industry journey.

VOICES OF THE INDUSTRY:
RESPECT

Companies are people. It is many other things, of course, but at its core, any organization is a collection of people trying to do their best. When I first met Ron, we quickly moved off talking about our businesses and immediately started talking about people and the importance of culture in building and sustaining a successful company.

A key part of our story was a solid foundation of trust and respect.

We started building our business by asking those we have worked with for years to take a chance and join a start-up. We hired friends. It's a scary moment to grow beyond that friends network because you constantly worry about maintaining your culture and living up to the promises you made your friends as they joined. However, standing still is never an option.

We wanted to make sure our customers, coworkers, and potential new coworkers knew what we were about at our core. To do that we created our maxims (quirky guiding principles) to set guard rails as an anchor point for every decision we needed to make, so we knew what our beliefs were as a collection of people. We created eleven maxims (ten was too obvious; we needed different) to help chart that path forward. The first maxim we wrote down was "Do the right thing." There is a lot of gray area in life; however, we always felt we could quickly decide what is right and what is wrong.

Our eleven maxims became foundational, and we held ourselves accountable to them. Only with time did I realize that their success was rooted in trust, and respect. Our maxims showed direction, which allowed our teams to move, make decisions, and do so independently and quickly. Creating an environment that allows people to be their best and provides autonomy and speed while creating a sense of purpose was a great unintended consequence of creating eleven quirky guiding principles.

We see respect in Andesa's workplace manifested as a high level of professional courtesy. Teammates are sensitive to others' schedules, workloads, and time. They show up promptly to meetings, focus on the discussion, and eschew multitasking. Honest, transparent, and timely communications are the norm, delivered in a civil tone and focused on the business issue, not personal perceptions. Teammates avoid the tunnel vision of being task oriented, value personal relationships, and keep an open mind to actively listen and embrace different ideas. The talents of their colleagues are recognized, and they genuinely care about their well-being and regard them with fairness and dignity. The bottom line is that collaboration is all about building strong teams that value, respect, and trust each other.

Development of individuals through teaching, coaching, mentoring, training, and investing in their success was also a major theme of our respect sessions. Since most of our training is on-the-job development, the daily interplay among staff honors those in the group with greater experience and knowledge. On-the-job training provides the chance for both mentor and mentee to help others grow as individuals and to pass along the values of the firm from one team member to another. Sharing time and knowledge demonstrates a genuine interest in helping another grow.

I prefer the word "coach" to "manager" in this context, because I believe it better describes the expectations for the role of a respectful leader. A great coach teaches, trains, and invests in the personal growth of the individuals on the team. Mistakes are tolerated as teaching moments. The coach seeks to strengthen the team and seeks peak team performance. A respectful leader interacts well with the team, seeks to understand, and accepts the individual talents of each team member. They determine how best to utilize those talents within the construct of the team and the goals. Experience has taught me that leaders who place results first often achieve those goals in the short run. However, those leaders who emphasize culture, values, and environment create a system that produces long-term, replicable, and sustainable results.

As I pushed this concept of leader behaviors in the values focus group conversations, the team began to describe a healthy work environment as one in which they felt psychologically safe and felt encouraged to contribute. One of our staff mentioned that "when a leader has respect for their team—not just 'shows' respect but actually *has* respect—the person feels their contribution matters and thus puts more effort into doing their best work. When an employee feels their ideas and opinions are encouraged, respected, and valued, they sense they belong and are more likely to go the extra mile to contribute."

The key responsibility of a leader is to create an environment where employees are respected and valued. But as John Walker's excerpt reminds us, the leader's purpose is not to achieve the end of greater productivity or results. It is instead to genuinely care about the personal growth and development of the individuals on the team. Productivity and results will follow as a natural by-product.

Respectful leaders demonstrate esteem for the individual through open and timely communications. When leaders give their full attention to a conversation, listen to understand, and demonstrate empathy, they create strong and open relationships. The timely delivery of information that impacts individuals also demonstrates a high degree of respect. Leaders create clarity around expectations, directions, and goals, choosing words that impart as much information as possible.

Many in the sessions described patience, tolerance, and a willingness to help as examples of respect in action. A respectful leader who understands the unique talents and motivations of the individual

> When leaders give their full attention to a conversation, listen to understand, and demonstrate empathy, they create strong and open relationships.

can challenge and help them achieve a new goal, demonstrating respect for that individual in the process. Public praise and private, constructive feedback also demonstrate respect and breed trust and loyalty into the relationship.

When an employee offers a suggestion for improvement or, perhaps, commits an error, a leader is faced with a critical choice. The leader can make a deposit of respect or invalidate the employee and damage the relationship. I'm certain I have dismissed ideas out of hand that I found to be silly, confusing, or unrealistic at the time. I am equally certain I have not treated every error as a teaching moment and, likely, reacted negatively or placed blame. In many cases, I would say my words and actions were hurtful, condescending, and disrespectful. Consider the better, more respectful approach of embracing the suggestion or error with questions instead of opinions or comments. "Can you explain further?" "Tell me more." "Have you thought about this?" or "Have you considered this perspective?" These are much more respectful ways to address an issue and still validate and honor that employee.

As we talked about the broader Andesa ecosystem, our values focus groups came to appreciate the firm as a collective consciousness of the people in it. If we value respect between individuals, we should also value respect in all aspects of the business partner relationship. If *we* truly are the firm, then our values must transcend peer-to-peer interfaces with our clients and business partners.

This perspective breakthrough led to a change in Andesa's vision statement. The values Andesa had espoused were personal values. Respect is about relationships, and that must be between individuals. The corporation is a legal entity, but in and of itself, absent of the individuals who are employed there, it cannot respect another corporation or individual. Instead of identifying our values as corporate values going forward, our Forever Vision statement identifies the employees who possess these values, along with an ethical and encouraging environment, as the critical component of the firm. This is what defines Andesa.

To reflect this awareness, the employees began to use the hashtag #ItStartsWithMe. The company's values were not words on a wall, nor were they merely how we expected others (or the collective "we") to act. The values became very personal and began to be reflected in the expectation, responsibility, and definition of each of us as employee-owners.

Respect Turns Client Relationships into Partnerships

Respect for our clients is born from a desire to create true partnerships. In the Andesa ecosystem, our clients' success translates into our success. Our ability to help them grow and achieve their goals and potential translates into long and mutually beneficial relationships. Understanding their objectives and aligning our services and response is paramount to a respectful relationship. Some clients are growth-oriented, while some operate in a steady, non-core, run-off business environment. To be respectful, we must truly meet each client in their situation.

Client interactions are often measured by how a person perceives the value of the interaction. Value can be discerned in financial terms, time pressures, responsiveness, quality, delivery on commitments, how one owns their responsibility in the situation, etc. At Andesa, when we can align our values with our client's values and situation, we create a sense of partnership whereby we become an extension of that client's operations beyond a contractual relationship. In a sense, Andesa becomes part of the client's ecosystem, and the client becomes part of Andesa's. Both organizations benefit. One of the highest compliments Andesa has ever received is when one of our largest clients noted, "Andesa is the standard against which we measure all of our vendor relationships."

Our best relationships are strategic in nature, where we offer advisory perspectives to alleviate stress. We don't just try to help our clients; we truly want them to succeed. We listen to their concerns, issues, and goals to better understand how their priorities align to their bigger strategic picture. Open, honest communication lends itself to building trust and moves the relationship from merely transactional to one that feels like a real partnership.

There is a fine line between confidentiality and transparency, which must be navigated in each relationship and in the whole ecosystem. We honor client confidentiality and strive to not compare one client to another client. If they have given us permission to do so, we will share who our clients are but will not disclose what systems they use or which products are served by Andesa's systems. We work individually with clients to be transparent about how things work at Andesa—the whole process, not just the outcome. It is a commitment to respect that invites our clients into that environment: to talk through things together, to work through challenges, and to strive to constantly improve the relationship and the ecosystem. Andesa's team members practice respect with each other and bring that same level of professional courtesy to client interactions.

Our ecosystem is further strengthened as our clients gather every eighteen months at the Andesa Client Forum to learn more about developments at Andesa and in the industry as well. In keeping with our purpose to help our employee-owners and clients reach their full potential, we invest some sessions at each Client Forum in general leadership principles. As this program has reached its second decade, an increased willingness to share information to benefit the entire ecosystem has been cultivated among the group.

Clearly, those clients who openly engage in this relationship benefit with a stronger sense of partnership than those who view the Andesa relationship as transactional or "like a vendor."

I learned that how Andesa is perceived by the client sometimes challenges our staff. It is tough when a client challenges us. Not everyone operates from the same sense of respect and fairness. Here is an important point: no client in the ecosystem is obligated to abide by Andesa's values, but that doesn't nullify our obligation to adhere to those values. In fact, these moments are precisely when we need to look to and marshal those core behaviors most. Disrespect from a client in a situation doesn't warrant disrespect from Andesa in return.

Transparency in our communication and in our approach to partnership creates an environment of mutual respect. However, the company must also stand firm in its own sense of value to avoid allowing a client to take advantage of the firm. When a client exercises their economic-based leverage or is accusatory, attacking or blaming, it is important in those moments to take a deep breath, then objectively consider the situation from the client's point of view. By tapping into the value of respect, our people can muster the courage to be professional and hold themselves to a higher standard. Andesa's value of respect calls us to action—something to *do*, not demand or expect.

TO SUCCEED:

- Leaders must genuinely care about the personal growth and development of the individuals on the team.
- It is vital not to lose respect by acting counter to your values.
- Not everyone in the ecosystem is obligated to abide by the company's core values, but that does not mitigate our obligation to operate according to our own core values.

KEY QUESTIONS FOR REFLECTION:

- What can we do to ensure all are treated with respect?
- How can we show respect when not being respected?
- How can we continue to hold someone in high regard in the middle of an argument?

CHAPTER FOUR

Integrity

*The supreme quality for leadership is unquestionably
integrity. Without it, no real success is possible.*
—Dwight Eisenhower

The letter arrived at my desk bearing a postmark but no return address—and no signature. Its anonymous author revealed that a longtime Andesa employee had pled guilty to a nonviolent crime two decades ago. The writer questioned my integrity: How could I allow someone with a criminal record to work at Andesa while, at the same time, I promoted values-based leadership and expected my employees to honor those values?

Honestly, my first impulse was to wad it up and toss it into the trash. If the letter was sent from an employee-owner, anonymous accusations like this were not in keeping with our values of respect, courage, honesty, and responsibility. The right thing to do would have been to contact our corporate ethics hotline. But as distasteful as I found their choice, I had a responsibility to the company due to the nature of our business. We're subject to Department of Insurance and SEC regulations, and any allegation of criminality has to be taken seriously. Though the letter had not come through our ethics hotline, we chose to follow that well-defined investigative process to address the allegation.

I knew the employee in question; he had a stainless reputation for trustworthiness and reliability in the roles he had held. If, in fact, he'd made a mistake in his youth, it certainly didn't reflect the adult I knew at Andesa. But I could not allow my personal experience to bias my judgment—because that, too, would have been out of sync with our values. Integrity means to act in accordance with one's values. In this situation, Andesa had a responsibility to the other employees and to the ecosystem to ensure whatever action was taken was the appropriate response. We also needed to respect the individual involved.

I convened a small group of trusted advisors to talk through the myriad of potential issues and ramifications before any intervention. Human resources engaged legal counsel. Our board was informed and asked challenging questions.

After weighing the issues and approach, I met with the employee to discuss the situation. It wasn't an easy meeting. Understandably, he was embarrassed, upset, and, of course, concerned for his job. Yes, he admitted, he had indeed pled guilty to the crime at issue, had made appropriate restitution and served his probation. He'd tried to learn from the mistake he'd made, to grow and leave it in the past. But he'd worried for years that somehow his secret would come out. I explained that before we did anything, we needed to look at the matter through several different lenses: legal, values, and business and client relationships. I promised him that we'd keep the process transparent and that he'd be updated weekly on how it was proceeding.

You might be wondering how we came to hire someone with a criminal record in the first place, but in fact, at the time of this person's hiring, our job application didn't cover questions about criminal records or other legal issues, and we'd only begun background screens for new hires after his hiring date. This employee had not lied on his application nor had he somehow skirted the system. When Andesa made it standard procedure to do background checks on new hires, it also did an initial check on all current employees. However, this individual's issue had occurred outside the background look-back period. The law favors the applicant versus the employer when relying on background checks in the employment process, limiting consideration of a crime as it relates to the applicant's suitability for the job. The time period fell well outside any FINRA, SEC, or EEOC guidelines and regulations, and we believed the individual was well suited to perform his role and provide services under our contracts.

There was concern about treatment of the matter in accordance with the Violent Crime Control and Law Enforcement Act of 1994. This act prohibited certain felons from ever working in the business of insurance unless they received a written consent waiver from the insurance commissioner. As there has been little case law under this act, the language and law are often broadly interpreted. Andesa sought an anonymous advisory opinion from the Pennsylvania Insurance Department regarding applicability of the act to the situation. We also arranged, at Andesa's expense, for the employee to consult with a retired deputy insurance commissioner on the waiver application preparation and process. After going through the process, the Insurance Department determined a waiver on the situation was not necessary. The regulators permitted the employee to continue to work in the insurance business—a big relief for all concerned.

During the process, I also communicated with several of our clients for whom the employee had worked on projects. In the spirit of our partnership and the health of the Andesa ecosystem, I was as transparent as possible while still protecting the person's identity out of respect for the individual. Client check-ins were held every two to three weeks or so to keep them apprised of the situation as it progressed. While the clients expressed concern, they also understood the intricacies of the situation and didn't push for a particular outcome but waited for us to offer a solution. The conclusion of the Insurance Department waiver process settled the matter, and our clients agreed that no further action was necessary from their standpoint.

This changed the way we hired: we updated our policy on preemployment criminal history screens and expanded the scope to conduct ongoing random and rotational criminal background checks, including board members in the background check process. But, most importantly, Andesa lived its values and stood by a quality individual who'd paid his debt to society and was a valued member of our corporate family.

How Integrity Informs Our Actions

Our integrity is challenged when others question whether we're really walking the walk or just mouthing platitudes. The anonymous letter writer assumed there was only one lens through which this situation could be viewed—but in a values-driven environment, our main intent is creating an environment in which every one of us can reach our full potential, and integrity demands that we act in accord with that intent.

I commented in a previous chapter that respect is a verb; it's something we give. But integrity as a value is a noun; it is something we obtain. As our values focus groups wrestled to define integrity, they often cited the other Andesa values in their definition. We came to understand that integrity is the process by which we earn the trust and respect of others. We produce that trust and respect by ensuring our words and actions are consistent with our standards and beliefs.

> Integrity is the process by which we earn the trust and respect of others.

Surprisingly, in his book *Value from Values*, John Walker listed integrity as a core value but did not define the term. In speaking with the employees who were part of the values focus group conversations, he shared, "I think of personal integrity as a state of mind whereby the individual strives to do the right thing in all he or she does with little concern for the cost. Of course, the right thing is as the individual perceives right. Why 'strives to do' as opposed to 'does'? Because 'does' is out of reach for us as humans, but 'strives to do' is not. When I think of integrity, I see a picture of my father, whom I do not place on a pedestal but whom I honor without limit. He was a man, to me, of incalculable integrity."[8] Perhaps the role model of his father as a man of integrity was so strong that John did not feel the term required definition.

While integrity is defined as a firm adherence to a code of especially moral or artistic values, incorruptibility, soundness, and completeness, our team defined it to include "Doing the right thing. Doing what you say you will do. Owning our mistakes. Words and actions are one and the same—consistent with our values, standards, and beliefs." In other words, integrity may be considered achieved at

---

8   John Walker, *Value from Values: The Making of Andesa Services.*

Andesa by each team member performing consistently within an environment of honesty, respect, courage, initiative, and responsibility.

Competing Perspectives

If we agree that integrity means acting and living in accordance with our values, we must admit that integrity is complicated. Competing worldviews, whether in a personal or business environment, can cause others to judge us according to a moral code that's different than our own. To demonstrate and emphasize this challenge, our values focus groups began its work on integrity with an experiment in differing perspectives. Most of the time, these perspectives have no innate value as "right" or "wrong," so no moral superiority can be assigned to either position.

On a whiteboard was a list of two morally equivalent yet often competing perspectives: *vertical authority* versus *horizontal authority*; *ends* as compared to *means*; *innovation* versus *efficiency*; and *autonomy* contrasted against *collaboration*. Each values focus group member was called to the board with a sticky note to indicate their personal preference along the spectrum. In the second round, armed with a different color of sticky note, they were asked to identify where they believed their department operated most of the time. Finally, in the third round, with a third colored sticky in hand, they were asked to identify where, from their perspective, Andesa operated most of the time. As you can imagine, the result was a dazzling spectrum of colors on display when multiplied across thirty participants. The tallies are displayed in the table below. Shaded cells represent a grouping of approximately half or more of the respondents across a three-cell range.

AUTHORITY

VERTICAL: Vertical authority works best in organizations where quick decisions from the top need to be disseminated through-out the ranks as quickly as possible with very little questioning or deviation.

HORIZONTAL: Horizontal authority works best in organizations where employees need to buy in or "own" new ideas, products, or services.

					Neutral				
Personal	1	2	1	1	3	3	8	8	2
Department	3	2	2	4	2	6	2	7	1
Andesa	-	1	3	7	5	6	3	2	2

MOTIVATION

ENDS: Ends-oriented businesses are focused on the bottom line. Results, performance, and measurements are critical.

MEANS: Means-oriented organizations tend to be more prevalent in the nonprofit world or social sector, where caring for people tends to be the mission.

					Neutral				
Personal	-	-	2	7	5	1	6	3	5
Department	3	6	5	5	4	2	1	1	2
Andesa	-	4	2	4	7	5	4	2	1

STRATEGY

INNOVATION: Innovative organizations rely on staying ahead of the curve in new products, services, and delivery channels as a means to accomplish goals. This works well when efficiency is not hugely important.

EFFICIENCY: Efficient organizations are more concerned with quality, speed, and stability to produce results. Efficient organizations have a tendency to standardize as much as they possibly can.

					Neutral				
Personal	1	3	6	3	1	5	7	2	1
Department	-	1	2	4	4	5	7	4	2
Andesa	1	0	1	7	2	6	5	3	3

SOCIAL FUNCTION

AUTONOMOUS: Autonomous organizations are often groups of solo agents. People affiliate to offset expenses and perhaps share community, but collaboration is not really important.

COLLABORATIVE: Collaboration indicates a high need for thinking synergistically and systemically. Teams allow for the eradication of individual weaknesses. The whole is greater than the sum of the parts.

					Neutral				
Personal	-	0	3	3	2	6	6	2	7
Department	-	1	3	4	7	4	5	3	2
Andesa	-	2	-	0	5	9	8	1	3

This experiment resulted in much self-reflection, debate, and a greater awareness of how we, as individuals, view our values through different perspectives. One of the members commented that it surprised him how much his personal preferences differed from those of his department and the company. When I pointed out that he judged his perspectives through a moral lens, assuming his personal value reflection weighed more favorably than the same, equally moral choice, he saw that both were, in fact, honorable perspectives and that one's personal and company values could coexist within those perspectives.

The group began to appreciate how difficult and important this work of defining and aligning values from different perspectives could be for Andesa (or any company, for that matter). We all have personal preferences and styles. We use value judgments all the time to assess others and their actions. We should not necessarily seek *alignment*; instead, we need to learn to navigate through differences of perspective (style, preference, personal, departmental, organizational, situational need, etc.) and to embrace this diversity of thought as a way of strengthening the environment around us.

We also recognized that when we only consider values through our lens—from our perspective—we run the risk of attributing greater significance or moral standing to our interpretation of values and assigning an inferior worth to another viewpoint. When we try to simplify complex issues, "either/or thinking" often results. Either/or thinking assumes that only two options exist, which limits our ability to consider and benefit from alternatives. Either/or thinking closes us off from possibilities. Our group began to appreciate that seeking to understand all perspectives provides for a better environment. Clearly, a standard of absolute perfection was not realistic, yet it was necessary to operate under a high moral standard to be a person of integrity.

I believe that values need to run deep in an organization, that they can't simply be slogans and words on the wall but have to be the actual criteria by which we monitor and operate our enterprise. If our organization is to act with integrity, the question "What do our values tell us to do?" should be asked frequently, especially at our most vulnerable and challenging moments.

From an ecosystem standpoint, corporate integrity is judged by how closely our personal values align with the behaviors and actions of the company and within the moral framework of a broader community. For example, would you willingly do business with a person or company that lacked integrity? Probably not. Thus, isn't integrity considered a necessity to even be in the game? It seems interesting to me that Andesa, along with so many other companies, calls out the importance of integrity by listing it as one of our core values.

We do so because, more often than not, we encounter stories about the lack of integrity. In *Called to Lead*, author John MacArthur writes, "[M]odern society is suffering from a severe shortage of true leaders. The problem is closely related to the dramatic moral decline that has been systematically eating away at the foundation of our culture since (at least) the 1960s. Western society no longer values *character*—integrity, decency, honor, loyalty, truthfulness, purity, and other virtues."[9] As integrity can be described as doing the right thing even when no one's looking, great examples are often unspoken or unknown to more than a few close colleagues. That's why it's often easier to cite examples of lapses when teaching integrity, as compared to positive examples. As a certified public accountant, I have always taken pride in the integrity of my profession—but the Enron scandal

---

9   John MacArthur, *Called to Lead: 26 Leadership Lessons from the Life of the Apostle Paul* (Nashville: Thomas Nelson, 2004), 161.

and the 2001 collapse of Arthur Andersen, previously one of the Big Five firms, shook my faith.

Enron was one of the largest energy commodity companies in the world. Based in Houston, TX, Enron employed over twenty thousand people and was a darling of Wall Street and the media—having been recognized as "America's most innovative company" for six consecutive years by *Fortune* magazine. Respect ("treating others as we would like to be treated") and integrity ("we work with customers and prospects openly, honestly, and sincerely") were listed among Enron's core values.

But the reality of the culture was the words on the wall did not match the actions of the leaders of the firm. Enron was found to have systematically engaged in accounting fraud, leading to the collapse and bankruptcy of the firm as well as its auditors and consultants, Arthur Andersen. In the aftermath, Congress passed the Sarbanes-Oxley Act to protect investors from fraudulent financial reporting by corporations. It seems we could no longer expect integrity; we needed to legislate it into existence. Strict new rules were imposed on accountants, auditors, and corporate officers. How sad!

The Enron saga teaches us that the brand stands for the integrity of the company and can have major implications to the company's ecosystem. The reputation of a business may be its only sustainable competitive advantage. Professor Thomas Dunfee of the Wharton School notes, "A company that fails to take steps to produce a climate conducive to positive work-related, ethical attitudes may create a vacuum in which employees so pre-disposed may foster a frontier-style, everyone for themselves mentality."

> When integrity is gone, the whole ecosystem can be destroyed, and many people can be hurt along the way.

Thus, when integrity is gone, the whole ecosystem can be destroyed, and many people can be hurt along the way.

Simply writing your values on the wall or in your annual statement is not good enough. They must truly become part of the fabric of the individuals, the organization, and the ecosystem in which all operate. Who we recruit is always a question of character more than ability, because to us, integrity is that important a value toward which we strive.

Leadership and Organizational Integrity

What does integrity look like at the organizational level? One of my favorite definitions comes from author Patrick Lencioni in his bestseller *The Advantage*. Lencioni describes an organization with integrity as one that "is healthy—when it is whole, consistent, and complete, that is, when its management, operations, strategy and culture fit together and make sense. These include minimal politics and confusion, high degrees of morale and productivity, and very low turnover among good employees," a noble goal for which any leader should strive.[10] So what behaviors would we expect an integrity-based leader to model?

First and foremost, a commitment to the cause rather than personal ambition can be a leader's best attribute. At Andesa, that means commitment to the growth of our employee-owners. It means investing in the relationship, understanding the whole individual and providing support and opportunity.

---

10 Patrick Lencioni, *The Advantage: Why Organizational Health Trumps Everything Else in Business* (San Francisco: Jossey-Bass, 2012), 5.

Secondly, leaders with integrity have an innate sense of right and wrong, and consistently stand up for what is right. They do not allow the magnitude of the opportunity or the potential consequences of the issue to override their principles. They ignore self-interest and come to the defense of those being wronged. They defend the weak and powerless and champion their cause. They value the good of the whole and build community, often at the expense of self-interest or what others think.

Finally, leaders must go first. Leaders who model integrity hold themselves to a higher standard than they expect of others. At a minimum, they must be committed to living and honoring the values subscribed to by the organization to which they belong. Effective leaders demonstrate a high degree of self-awareness and can acknowledge their own flaws. I also notice that people of integrity embrace lifelong self-improvement. In doing so, they inspire others to embrace their own potential. Employees reward such leaders with confidence, support, and respect. Dwight Eisenhower's quote at the beginning of this chapter bears repeating here: "The supreme quality for leadership is unquestionably integrity. Without it, no real success is possible."

How does the industry appreciate integrity? Over the years I've had many occasions to interact with Ron Laeyendecker, senior VP of executive benefits at Protective. I value Ron's perspectives on the market and often seek his insights to inform my planning. I asked him to share some personal reflections on the importance of integrity to our industry.

VOICES OF THE INDUSTRY
INTEGRITY

Integrity is essential at all stages of a successful career and is something that grows and evolves continuously. Early in my career as a pricing actuary, integrity was critical when setting the large volume of pricing assumptions. There are no absolutes, no exactly correct assumptions. You need to do the right thing when setting those assumptions. And the company and customers need to trust you did the right thing when setting the prices. Doing the right thing and building trust are two attributes often found when attempting to define integrity.

As my career continued and included sales and operations, I have noticed that defining integrity has become more challenging. Every transaction involves multiple "customers," including clients, advisors, staff, management and shareholders. Balancing the diverse needs of each customer often creates solutions that may be viewed as suboptimal by all parties. Integrity now must evolve to adapt to differing points of view. Transparency, open communication, and sharing of information becomes critical to building trust. Sharing how our products work, what assumptions we've used, and what the financial implications of changes to the product look like has allowed me to build strong relationships with many customers over the years. They may not have liked the answers at times, but the transparency allowed them to see that our actions and our words were aligned.

The life insurance business is one of the most complex businesses we have today. The segment of executive benefits markets is even more complicated. With that comes a heightened requirement for integrity. I've heard many times that advisors won't sell your product and clients won't buy your products if they don't trust you or your company. Generating sales involves a long lead time as you slowly build trust with the advisors and then build trust with their clients. Insurance carriers understand how important integrity is to their business. In both carriers I've worked for, you will see references to trust, integrity, doing the right thing, and serving people in their published value statements. One even had integrity as a discussion item in our annual performance review.

It's not always easy to do the right thing in business. You will often be presented with situations that are completely legal, above board, and endorsed by colleagues or managers but ultimately are not the right thing to do. It's what you do in those moments that shape your career.

As I reflect on integrity, both personally and professionally, I believe you come into a career with an innate sense of right and wrong. Over time, this evolves and adapts to reflect the nuances of the business world. The insurance business is still a relationship-driven business. Without trust, you cannot build relationships. And without integrity, you cannot build trust.

Andesa's clients operate with their own perspectives on integrity. As I've noted, life insurance is a noble industry, largely populated by good people who care about their clients. I have witnessed many administrative errors that have resulted in the insurance company bearing the loss for the misstep and making the client whole. Open and transparent communications are paramount when dealing with people of integrity. Sticking with the truth is a core principle, even when it's not in someone's best economic interests to do so. Over the years, being truthful with clients and prospects has cost us money and opportunity, but we accept those short-term losses in exchange for the long-term reputational and relationship gains.

Confidential information is treated as a sacred trust in a healthy ecosystem. As a partner, we are often privy to proprietary information before it becomes public. I can't begin to count the number of calls I have had with clients over the years who have given me a heads up on something and asked that I keep it confidential—sometimes asking that I do not even share it with my team. Internally, we operate with a "need to know" approach with client data and information. As CEO, there is information I do not have access to, simply because I do not need to know it to carry out my responsibilities. While we appreciate honesty and transparency in our communications, maintaining confidentiality is another hallmark of integrity. Imagine how Andesa would suffer if our clients could not trust us with confidential information.

Or imagine what their impression of Andesa would be if we consistently missed commitments and deadlines. Proposals on new business are fraught with this risk. The proposal process is complex; many elements must be considered when a project is defined, scoped, and estimated for costs and timelines. This process is often done under time constraints to determine if the project would even be green-lighted under a corporate budget. As a good partner, Andesa has the obligation to include a caveat in estimates, in terms of the confidence we have in the accuracy based on the best information at the time the estimate was created. As requirements are finalized or changed, Andesa has the responsibility to communicate the changes and impact on the project from the original assumptions. These are often challenging conversations to initiate, but when they're handled professionally by relationship and project managers, they build trust and strengthen the relationship and ecosystem.

How would our clients react if we consistently made errors and shifted the blame to our clients or other colleagues? It takes integrity to acknowledge our mistakes to our clients; it's not easy, but it's absolutely necessary! To support the ecosystem, each partner must own their own behavior and their work. The importance of aligning our personal values and our company's values with other companies and players in the ecosystem cannot be underestimated if the entire industry is to have integrity.

A final reflection on integrity as it applies to our purpose at Andesa: as we work on behalf of our clients and employee-owners to ensure they achieve their full potential, we acknowledge that this objective is beyond the immediacy of pure role and contractual business objectives. It takes real courage to not compromise your actions because of the situation or to use circumstances to justify your actions. Helping clients and employee-owners grow in integrity requires developing the wherewithal to strive for a higher standard than what's commonly accepted. Consultant and author Adam Grant paints an integrity journey image for us to embrace: "I'd love to live in a world where people spend as much time developing their character as they do on developing their careers. What if our moral codes were as clear as our ambitions? Goals without values are empty."[11]

Integrity is a challenging value to uphold, creating tremendous expectations on us as individuals. I'm grateful that Andesa calls us

---

11   Adam Grant (@AdamMGrant), Twitter, September 16, 2020, https://twitter.com/AdamMGrant/status/1306310690462986240.

to live a life of integrity as we strive to reach our full potential. In the next chapter, we'll examine Andesa's value of courage—a value that helps us ignite the actions our values demand.

TO SUCCEED:

- Integrity is the process by which we earn the trust and respect of others. We produce that trust and respect by ensuring our words and actions are consistent with our values, standards, and beliefs.
- Leaders who model integrity hold themselves accountable to a higher standard than they expect of others.
- Integrity-based leaders let their values be their guide. They consistently stand up for what is right.

KEY QUESTIONS FOR REFLECTION:

- Is integrity something you ever master, or is it an everyday journey toward success where every test is a step in the right or wrong direction? Is our integrity only measured by our last test?
- Are you treating others as you want to be treated?
- Is your integrity more valuable than money or power?

CHAPTER FIVE

Courage

It is curious that physical courage should be so common
in the world and moral courage so rare.
—Mark Twain

If we define courage as acting in alignment with our moral code even when it puts us in danger of loss, then the unanimous vote by Andesa's founders, management, and owners in December 2019 was surely among the most courageous acts in our company's history.

Andesa had ownership transition alternatives. For several years leading up to the ESOP, we'd had conversations with friends of the firm about possible shareholder succession. Private equity and venture capital firms often reached out to discuss investment or acquisition. A sale to a strategic buyer would likely have maximized the return on company value to the exclusive benefit of the shareholders.

But these options conflicted with our commitments to our employees and our clients. We realized we would be better served over the long term by remaining independent and self-governed, with the ownership benefits of the firm accruing to the employee-owners who serve the company. The fact that our major clients are large insurance companies with a long-term outlook and a vested interest in Andesa's longevity as an independent company further strengthened the argument in favor of preserving the ecosystem.

Walking the Walk

Values are just words if you don't have the courage to live them, and the 100 percent ESOP decision was in alignment with the company's people-first vision. The owners showed their courage by exchanging their ownership position for a creditor position to finance the ESOP transaction. That speaks volumes about their commitment to the values of the company. Many more Andesa families now share in the ownership and vision because of the ESOP transition. They and our clients can continue to see Andesa endure.

If the transfer of 100 percent ownership to the employees through the ESOP was courageous, then certainly the founding of the company decades earlier was also a story of courage and perseverance.

A doctor of economics, John Walker was in his eleventh year as an associate professor of economics and director of the computing center at Lehigh University when he was approached by the principals of Covert and Associates. Covert's primary business was financial counseling to executives, along with the design and operation of supplemental benefit plans, and the firm was facing serious technical and strategic challenges. John joined Covert in 1978, primarily to construct Monte Carlo simulations and executive benefits computer models for them. Within a year, a fresh crisis arose as a result of a dispute with the company's external partner. The external partner operated a critical administrative system for life insurance–driven benefits that had been developed for the firm. That administrative system was now in jeopardy of not being available. Without that system, a major part of the company's business would disappear.

The company was in trouble. It had to have an alternative system to administer the business before the external partner pulled the plug on the current system. John knew little about the development of a life insurance system and, based upon his rough estimates for building this highly complex application, he did not think it was possible to complete the task in time to save the business. However, he knew he had to try. He didn't know it then, but he was embarking on the creation of a solution that would lead to the formation of a new company called Andesa Services.

Contractually, Covert had access to the source code for the administrative system, but there was little to no written documentation. In addition, there were few, if any, subject matter experts on staff. John set out to reverse engineer the system and learn the necessary administrative processes under the pressure of a save-the-business deadline. The wretched condition of the system turned out to be a blessing. Six months of intense digging and drudgery taught John more about this insurance/benefits system than he probably would have ever discovered under more favorable circumstances.

Dr. Walker learned two critical lessons through this exercise: (1) The basic framework of the current system was fundamentally flawed. Numbers did not tally from year to year, and it was not always clear what they meant. (2) The tax-advantaged, financial vehicles administered by the system had the potential to be highly effective tools for the company's clients. After an exhaustive analysis of the software,

John initiated a project to construct a superior system from scratch, complete with documentation and user involvement.

There were financial stresses and many sleepless nights. The principals considered abandoning the effort on several occasions but stuck with their bold commitment to sustaining the business. This created the relationships in the ecosystem, which carried them through trials that tested their moral courage.

Nine months after beginning the project, the company's largest client was up and running with a totally new set of comprehensive reports. The system was completed in half the estimated time—barely in time to avoid the collapse of Covert and Associates. The new system didn't just work, it worked brilliantly. The client checked for errors but found none. Client personnel finally understood the nuances of the benefit plans designed for their unique needs. The company had a product it could be proud of, one that came much closer to giving the client what they needed than the original. Decades later, Andesa is part of the life insurance ecosystem, with seven of the top thirteen life insurance companies in the country listed among its clients.

Our founder inspires courage. In *Value from Values*, he writes, "In an ethical environment, courage is promoted. The firm stands behind its people in the hard choices they make … But when you know that you will be backed up by those around you, even the hardest choices and actions become doable." Aristotle called courage the first virtue because it makes all other virtues possible, and John went on to note that "without courage to back up one's view and initiative to follow through, the powerful qualities of honesty, respect, integrity, and responsibility will lie dormant."[12]

The courage we talk about at Andesa is moral courage, the strength to do the right thing despite risk, challenge, ridicule, or

---

12   John Walker, *Value from Values: The Making of Andesa Services.*

personal loss. As we often say, "Growth occurs outside your comfort zone," especially when dealing with a new opportunity or an uncomfortable situation. But when we're willing to step out and step up to take this risk, backed up by a supportive environment, then one by one, little by little, we begin to demonstrate corporate courage and create something bigger and bolder.

It takes courage to show respect and compassion to others. It takes courage to act with integrity. If respect and integrity place incredible demands on us, courage gives us the convictions to meet those demands. It takes courage to speak the truth when a lie might be easier. It takes courage to start something new, to move outside your comfort zone and demonstrate initiative. It takes courage to be responsible for others and to a team, to put others' needs ahead of our own.

> If respect and integrity place incredible demands on us, courage gives us the convictions to meet those demands.

"If I Only Had the Nerve ..."

A quick Google image search on "courage" will reveal lion photos within the first couple of search results. The legendary depiction of the lion as a symbol of courage is what makes L. Frank Baum's depiction of the Cowardly Lion in *The Wizard of Oz* such an effective oxymoron, because you don't expect a lion to be a scaredy cat. I think we relate to the character because we've all had moments when our courage has been tested—yet, like the Lion, we've gone forward toward the threat, rather than beat a retreat.

We discussed *The Wizard of Oz* and the Cowardly Lion to energize the values focus groups' discussions about this value. The group observed that a mindset focused on fears and failures was a poor starting point. The Lion lacked self-confidence because he'd lost touch with his true nature. How many of us do the same thing? We let some disappointment or challenge feed head trash, starving our sense of self-worth. We engage in an internal dialogue about potential consequences and often assume the worst, instead of focusing our energy on the possible successful outcomes. More energy is created when we focus on what we are building and creating and moving toward than when we focus on and emphasize the problems or issues we face. The right mindset and a supportive environment activate our talents. The Lion transforms from a coward cringing in the forest to a medal-wearing hero recognized by the Wizard.

The group also noted that the Lion became stronger as he received support from his Oz companions. Working toward a common goal creates a communal sense of purpose and a commitment to one another. While the Lion might not have been able to summon up the nerve on his own, he stormed the Witch's castle with his friends when it meant saving Dorothy. Being part of the team raised his sagging self-esteem and self-awareness as he realized he'd had courage all along. Many of us lack the self-discipline and willpower to accomplish our goals, but we will find the inner fortitude if it means not disappointing our friends, colleagues, or family.

The group also learned the importance of networking and mentors. Dorothy's belief and encouragement inspired the Lion to believe in himself. If you research the past of almost any successful individual, you'll find they had partners pushing them, coaching them, depending on them, and cheering for them. The support of others is a perpetual source of motivation from which we can draw when faced with challenges that might otherwise feel insurmountable.

As our values focus groups shifted from the make-believe land of Oz to how courage is experienced at Andesa, I was curious why they thought courage was needed as a value at all. I mean, we develop software and provide services to life insurance companies; what's so courageous about that? I could understand if we were a police department, fire department, or emergency room—but Andesa?

The employee-owner responses revealed how our RICHIR values are in fact the values of our staff as well as our company. The group described courage as the glue that holds all the values together. They noted how courage is the root word of encourage. They described courage as a gift of inspiration, as the secret sauce that emboldens us to do what looks impossible. And they noted that the pursuit of our Andesa Forever Vision will demand change and evolution over time, requiring corporate and individual courage as we venture into our future.

Andesa values people who are ready to challenge the status quo in pursuit of a better way. When these innovations and challenges are about the process and the business, incremental breakthroughs strengthen the ecosystem and provide tremendous value. Innovation is some combination of courage and curiosity. Yet, in many environments, a person must dig deep to summon enough courage to question the status quo. In contrast, thanks to our values-based environment where individuals are respected, we often see less experienced developers making significant contributions through their questions and suggestions. I'd be kidding myself if I believed that their suggestions are never met with the typical "that's not the way things are done here" response, but I do believe we have an environment that encourages the conversations. That's a testimony to the courage and integrity of our more experienced architects, who welcome these improvement discussions with little defensiveness but with a desire to learn and improve themselves.

Many risk-averse cultures limit an employee's ability to use their own judgment. In their search for "lean and mean," many companies apply manufacturing principles to knowledge-based work. While Andesa operates with some repetitive process and control environments designed for our service offerings, much of what we produce in our technology deliverables are unique solutions to meet client expectations. As such, asking for help at Andesa is a sign of strength, not weakness. We try to encourage "above-the-line behavior," where employee-owners act on the decisions they make within their scope and authority without constantly checking with leads or managers. I can usually predict project success (quality, timeliness, economics) by how a team performs against this above-the-line standard. If a project team is enthusiastic, passionate, and energized, success is likely. Conversely, below-the-line behavior (always asking what to do) usually manifests itself in cynicism, pessimism, and a lack of energy on the project team and results naturally suffer. Fortunately for us, the former is much more prevalent.

Our Security Incident Response Program is another values-based behavior example of courage in action. Our risk-management team encourages employees who become aware of any security issue to promptly report it. Timeliness is often of the essence in such matters, so negative consequences or damage can be stopped or mitigated if problems are caught early on. Most security incidents reported in our program are self-reported errors such as the sending of sensitive data to an incorrect email. Andesa's security auditor, Ryan Scanlan, noted, "Employees did not hesitate to raise their hand and admit they had made a mistake. They showed **courage** in pointing out their own errors, regardless of the potential fallout. They demonstrated **honesty** and **integrity** by not sweeping the incident under the rug and hoping no one noticed. They took **responsibility** for the incident and took the **initiative** to report it so that it could be handled appropriately." Courage gives us the confidence and strength to live our values, even when the possibility of negative consequences exists.

The values focus group also noted how courage and honesty work in conjunction to create a healthy environment. We often use adjectives like *intentional, purposeful, radical,* or *candid* to describe difficult and challenging conversations. These conversations are uncomfortable because we understand that the person being called out may react defensively. When the conversation becomes personal, the resulting conflict is unhealthy. But honest and courageous conversations conducted in a healthy manner about ideas, processes, and business challenges often lead to breakthroughs and improvements. These are the interactions we seek to encourage in a values-based system.

How Does a Courageous Leader Behave?

I was introduced to Matt O'Mara, one of the cofounders of Spraoi, a machine learning insurtech company, as we joined together in pursuit of a business opportunity. Similar to Andesa's founding story, I was impressed with his team's entrepreneurial courage and asked that he share some of his personal reflections on courage in our industry.

VOICES OF THE INDUSTRY
COURAGE

Courage can be found everywhere in our society, with our military and first responders immediately coming to mind. We think of courage and see US troops approaching Omaha Beach or firefighters and police officers running toward the Twin Towers consumed in flames. Suffice to say, while entrepreneurship doesn't require the same type of courage, it does require courage of a different kind: the courage to persevere. That courage can be tested many times through the journey of entrepreneurship.

THE COURAGE TO TRUST:

At the outset of the entrepreneurial journey, the founding team of Spraoi learned a great deal about trust. We left successful individual careers in the pursuit of the shared vision. While early wins racked up and success was coming, we began to scale aggressively to meet demands, which required us to bring in new people. The founders took a big risk and trusted one another. We now had to have the courage to trust more and more people, some of whom we knew, some we didn't. It was a leap of faith; some were home runs, but not everyone worked out perfectly. What got us through the ups and downs of the journey was the courage to trust. We trusted in what we were setting out to do and in what we were building, and we now trusted others to help us grow the dream.

THE COURAGE TO STICK TO YOUR GUNS:

Entrepreneurism is also about the courage to stick to your plan and approach when you believe that you are right and have the courage to see things through. One of our first clients, who took a chance on us, purchased our product. Unlike most products, machine learning products require a covenant between the provider and the client. When they were not using it to the level required for it to produce results, we decided we had to intercede. We did so at the risk of losing revenue, losing the client as a reference, and exposing ourselves to negative market perception. Our courage to act, and the tact to do so in a way that would mitigate downside risk to the extent possible, was tested. We weathered that and countless other decisions that tested our resolve along the way: sticking with employees who were learning about products and services, saying no to work outside our core competency in pursuit of revenue, among others. The courage to stick to our guns has fueled the growth of our core assets.

THE COURAGE TO PIVOT:

While sticking to your guns is important, you also need to have the courage to take on new opportunities sometimes. After eighteen months in business, we realized that our software-as-a-service machine learning business was not going to be as profitable as originally planned (due to the peculiarities of insurance data quality). We had two options: the easy way (reprice going forward) or the more difficult way (pivot our business and investment to another way of delivering at our original price point). The difficult way was going to require innovation that could only be realized through significant time and investment. While there was no guarantee innovation would work, we had confidence. We measured the courage of our decision in the subsequent eighteen months and hundreds of thousands of dollars in reinvestment (profits from the business, not additional funding). We felt vindicated for our courage in the pivot with the production license of Barrel (our machine learning platform) in Q3 of this year.

There are numerous instances where people have bravely used their courage to achieve more than build a new company. Courage has resulted in lives saved from drowning and from burning buildings. However, there are acts in everyday life as well, even in the (comparatively) mundane world of insurtech.

Courageous leaders put others ahead of self. They don't need or seek adulation. They don't shy away from criticism but understand it comes with the responsibility of leadership. Courageous leaders prioritize the growth of their team in the long term against the short-term pressures on results—often absorbing the heat for the team during their learning cycle. Those leaders are supportive but also challenge their team to reach its full potential. They are willing to engage in the difficult work and difficult conversations alongside their team.

> A courageous leader approaches challenges with a collaborative attitude rather than a command-and-control mindset.

A courageous leader approaches challenges with a collaborative attitude rather than a command-and-control mindset. They are open to thoughts, ideas, and opinions of others and actively seek them out. They challenge the team to observe, study, and recommend solutions. They excel at coaching and engaging others on the team and across the organization with difficult work. But they also understand that leadership is not a popularity contest. They seek input and build consensus but make decisions based on what's best for the team and the organization versus any individual employee or their own popularity.

When I was a young man just starting out in my career, the 1977 *Harvard Business Review* article "Managers with Impact: Versatile and Inconsistent" by C. Wickham Skinner and W. Earl Sasser significantly influenced my approach to leadership.[13] We expect our leaders to be consistent, and we take comfort in this persistent, predictable environment. But business is not predictable, and the environment is not constant but ever changing. Each client and colleague is unique, with individual needs and expectations. The paradox is that situational leadership is needed to navigate the complexities of the world. Yet so many leaders only learn and use a small array of approaches and skills repeatedly. Too often we hear the truism, "If all you have is a hammer, every problem looks like a nail." That kind of tunnel vision results in leadership and organizational inertia.

Courageous leaders are situational leaders. They are deeply consistent in their values, beliefs, and the commitment to the vision, even as pressure mounts. But they adapt to the circumstances at hand in everything else. They constantly learn and apply new approaches and techniques to various situations. They immerse themselves in detail in some matters and stay highly strategic in others. They demand urgency in some situations and show patience in others. They are sometimes supportive and other times sharp and challenging. They can make quick decisions in urgent cases and demand more data

---

13   C. Wickham Skinner and W. Earl Sasser Jr., "Managers with Impact: Versatile and Inconsistent," *Harvard Business Review* (November 1977).

and analysis in others. They have high expectations for some experienced team members and are more tolerant and observant while developing others. They delegate authority in some circumstances and retain task responsibilities in other areas.

Finally, courageous leaders take risks, but they take calculated risks. It's a risk-management versus risk-avoidance mentality. This type of risk-taking develops courage over time through multiple trial-and-error lessons. Of course, leadership at Andesa is not intended to be experienced as an adrenaline-pumping thrill ride. Our clients value stability, reliability, and accuracy. Therefore, we appreciate thoughtful and thorough analysis before action. Data, planning, and analysis rule the day. When a leader encourages new ideas and pursues a new course, they understand that the likelihood of success more than compensates for taking the risk in the first place. It doesn't mean the organization will shy away from a challenge or difficult situation. Calculated risk implies the steps forward will be purposeful to advance the organization in alignment with its purpose and toward its strategic vision.

Client Relationships and Courage

First and foremost, our relationships are built on trust, honesty, and integrity. This requires the courage to do the right things consistently, without regard to the personal or business consequence—even when things aren't going right. That sometimes leads to tough conversations, but owning our responsibility in the situation and collaborating to resolve the issue is a good foundation for customer service and a long-term, respectful relationship.

When bad things happen, I circle back with our clients after the issue is resolved to ensure our commitment to the relationship.

If our purpose includes striving to help our clients achieve their full potential, I like to lean in and push through the situation to continue to build and strengthen the ecosystem. The good news is, I don't need to have these conversations too often. The bad news from our client's perspective is that the conversations need to happen at all. But over time, I believe our clients appreciate the openness and reassurance of how much we value the relationship.

As we think about our purpose to help both our employee-owners and our clients reach their full potentials, we recognize that courage activates all other values. We have to be willing to step outside our comfort zone to experience growth. Courage lets us put aside our concerns and fears, freeing us to act. Courage can appear in our tragedies, our successes, and throughout our personal and professional journey. And it's courage that drives us to persevere through the days and weeks when the outcomes are uncertain. I, for one, am grateful Andesa built courage into its value lexicon.

TO SUCCEED:

- Values are just words if you don't have the courage to live them.
- Courage provides the motivation to embrace change, lead boldly, act decisively, and create more energy for good.
- Courageous leaders are situational leaders. They are consistent in their values and beliefs but adapt to the circumstances of the environment in everything else.
- Courageous leaders take risks, but they take calculated risks. Data and analysis are imperative.

KEY QUESTIONS FOR REFLECTION:

- Is courage about being true to yourself?

- What risk level are you willing to accept?

- How do you convince yourself to act when you are scared?

CHAPTER SIX
Honesty

*[B]ut I see nothing in this renewal of the game of "Robin's alive"
but a general demoralization of the nation, a filching from
industry its honest earnings, wherewith to build up palaces,
and raise gambling stock for swindlers and shavers, who are too
close to their career of piracies by fraudulent bankruptcies. My
dependence for a remedy, however, is in the wisdom which grows
with time and suffering. Whether the succeeding generation is to
be more virtuous than their predecessors I cannot say; but I am
sure they will have more worldly wisdom, and enough, I hope, to
know that honesty is the 1st chapter in the book of wisdom.*
—Thomas Jefferson to Nathaniel Macon, January 12, 1819

I'd met up with Bob Waks, CEO of the Training Center for Sales
and Business Development, one day over a cup of coffee at Starbucks

because Andesa had a problem we couldn't seem to solve. Put bluntly, we sucked at sales.

Our talented team excelled at problem-solving, solution building, relationships, and customer service—but a sales capabilities assessment indicated we scored in the bottom third percentiles for everything other than our presentation approach—and handling rejection. We'd become really good with rejection because we'd had plenty of practice. The tactical strategy of injecting an expert into the ecosystem had not yielded any progress over the years. We'd tried hiring insurance technology sales experts into the organization but met with little to no success and much internal consternation. It was time for a new approach.

I told Bob that we'd selected Jerry Pennella, then a business analyst working within the company, to lead the charge because his strengths—communication, being futuristic, being an achiever, an includer, and a maximizer—looked to me like the ideal combination to drive our business development experiment. He had the right values, understood our systems, and had experienced the Andesa ecosystem from the client viewpoint. When he accepted the challenge, I wanted to ensure Jerry had the opportunity to reach his full potential. Now I needed to engage a sales coach to help him succeed. I asked Bob if he would be willing to take on the responsibility for Jerry's training.

Bob shot me down with his brutally honest response.

"I won't do it," he said, in a tone that left no room for argument. "I won't do it unless you agree to participate in the training as well."

He must have seen the look on my face, because Bob went on to explain that sales isn't transactional but relational in nature. It is about the building of trust connections that result in two individuals or organizations working together to solve problems. Without prompting, Bob explained how David Sandler's core values of honesty, integrity, and respect help in building relationships. Because of our values alignment, the Sandler methodology appealed to me and appeared to be the right fit. Listening to him, I understood that if Andesa was going to improve our sales prowess, we were going to have to do so by purposefully addressing our entire ecosystem, not just by inserting something new into the ecosystem and hoping for a better result.

Was I thrilled at the thought of taking sales training? Well, no—but I respected Bob's frankness and recognized he was the right fit to partner with us. And yes, I did agree to participate in the sales training to get the ball rolling.

That training has resulted in an increased growth trajectory and expansion at Andesa plus a mutually beneficial professional relationship for both of us. I am grateful to call Bob a friend as well as an advisor.

I believe in the concept of virtuous business. Through my experience in nonprofit organizations, I've found decisions are often based on the organizations' mission but frequently at the expense of margin. My responsibility in those organizations was to ensure an adequate margin to continue the mission as long as there was need—in other words, forever. I see similar perspectives with our clients, as life insurance companies are there to meet people's needs at often their most vulnerable and challenging times. Many of our insurance company clients have one-hundred-plus-year histories of providing value and comfort to families and businesses in their hours of need.

Thomas Jefferson's remarks about business at the beginning of this chapter are cautionary. However, his inspiration to us and future generations is to be virtuous. He begins by encouraging honesty—it is that important to a virtuous business.

Let me be honest with you: I've had more than one coach or mentor tell me that when I say, "Let me be honest with you," it implies

I've been dishonest or at least not transparent up to that point. They point out that the phrase I should say instead is that "I want to make an important point" or "I am going deeper into details than perhaps I am ordinarily comfortable with." Lesson learned—and it's one I regularly share with teammates and mentees.

It Starts with Honesty

The first value our values focus groups tackled was honesty. The homework for our sessions included excerpts from John Walker's book *Value from Values*. From our founder's definition, we understood that we were challenged to a higher definition of honesty at Andesa:

> *In an ethical environment, not only are people honestly respected, honesty is valued above all else. The culture focuses on honesty, not because it will bring a profit or please the client but simply and solely because it is the right thing to do. The individual is given great power in an environment where people are expected to be honest. The subterfuge of turning a blind eye to lying, cheating, stealing, trickery, or any other kind of dishonesty in the name of attaining a goal effectively undermines the individual's desire to do good by creating competing loyalties. Alternatively, in an environment that sincerely promotes honesty, the individual is free to be truthful, even if the truth may have costs for the organization. A hard truth, by definition, is not easy. It is the man reporting the whereabouts of his dangerous brother to the authorities. It is the coach giving his new quarterback time on the field, possibly losing the game, because he promised the young man that he would play. It is the new data entry personnel going to her boss and admitting that she just deleted three days of records, even if the error could not be traced back*

to her. Within a supportive environment, doing the right thing still may not be easy, but it is respected.[14]

On the surface, honesty seems to be a gateway value—you won't be hired unless you are honest. Most people claim to be honest and are, for the most part, honest individuals. Thus, a company shouldn't need to chalk up honesty as a value. Right?

And yet, since each of us will most likely attest to our own honesty, why do we normally prefer to respond anonymously to employee surveys? Whether this stems from fear of reprisal or a wish to avoid difficult conversations, we inherently understand that honesty comes at a price. Therein lies the conundrum. If we expect our employees, our leaders, and ultimately our company to be honest, we must proclaim it and uphold it as a value, especially when it may require paying a price.

> If we expect our employees, our leaders, and ultimately our company to be honest, we must proclaim it and uphold it as a value, especially when it may require paying a price.

Most of us can recall times when honesty hurt us on our business journey. Perhaps our honesty was viewed by leaders as insubordination or cancerous negativity, resulting in exclusion from opportunities or missed salary increases or promotions. Maybe honest feedback resulted in damaged relationships.

Have you ever been honest with a prospective client about budget estimates or project duration and lost an order as a result? Honesty in those situations is tough, especially if we assume the competition

---

14 John Walker, *Value from Values: The Making of Andesa Services.*

is playing by a different set of rules. We have all probably competed against companies that underestimate costs and commit to deadlines to win the business. They fully expect to renegotiate on the back end when the project runs long and is over budget. Seasoned clients who have been scarred by such experiences become tainted and begin to view every provider of service with the same skepticism. This institutionalized lack of honesty destroys partnership relationships and makes each interaction a transactional exchange of commodities.

Little by little we come to expect that's the way "business is done"—the way the game is played. We begin to understand what is necessary to get by, to get ahead, to win the deal, to succeed, and in so doing, we chip away at our honesty without even recognizing it. If I'm being honest, being honest is hard.

So as we Andesa employee-owners began our values journey, I chose honesty to begin our conversations. If the result of our work was to get to the heart of our company, our employees needed to be honest with leadership and with each other. I understood and appreciated the importance of creating an environment in which my colleagues felt safe enough to be honest, even when it was tough. I used two methods to accomplish this.

As facilitator, I established the ground rules for our sessions. While the obvious expectations of "come prepared, no distractions, everyone participate," etc. were among our guidelines, I added #NotMyPresident to encourage honesty. It was a timely and clever play on the social media trend of the day but with a significantly different meaning. Even though I was facilitating the conversations, it was important to suspend my CEO status during these meetings. Our goal was to perform a true and thorough assessment of Andesa's values. We required honesty, so the team needed to feel safe.

If the group had tough criticisms of Andesa, our leadership team, or my personal leadership, and they were met with defensiveness or countered with how wrong and misguided those perceptions might be (and believe me, there were many times when that was my first inclination), the dialogue would have shut down. It might even have felt good to correct a misconception in the short run—but it would have sent the message that being honest at Andesa has negative consequences. #NotMyPresident was not only a ground rule for our participants, it served as a reminder of my commitment to the process and to the group.

The second method used to create the safe environment for our discussions on honesty was to model the behaviors of an honest environment. This eventually became known as the Pizza Experiment.

In establishing our meeting times, I scheduled two of the three group sessions over the lunch hour. It's common at Andesa to provide food if a meeting is scheduled over lunch. Yet lunch was not ordered for either of the first two meetings. As folks gathered in the conference room for our initial session about the ground rules and to review the work on which we were about to embark, the puzzled looks were intermingled with disappointed glances and an occasional comment of "Where's the pizza?" or "I thought there would be food." As we gathered for our sessions to dive into the honesty discussion, again, there was no pizza—to everyone's evident disbelief and frustration. Before we engaged in our honesty conversation, I kickstarted the dialogue with the Pizza Experiment questions:

Was there an expectation that lunch would be provided for the meeting? Is there a policy or handbook requirement that lunch be provided? Have any of the values of Andesa been violated if the manager fails to provide lunch? If yes, which ones and how? What does this discussion have to do with the vision and values effort in which our focus groups are engaged?

With an opportunity to have an open and honest conversation about a real-time, less-threatening issue facing the group (primarily hunger and disappointment in their facilitator), the group was able to appreciate the concept of values not only from a personal perspective but from the perspective of others.

The Pizza Experiment challenged us to consider alternate points of view and why different expectations existed—prior employer policy, location of the participants (whether they are in a remote office or working from home), different start times (not everyone eats lunch at noon), whether they'd volunteered for the group or had been assigned the work by their manager, etc. And while less than half the participants expected lunch to be provided, the bigger issue became how the expectations for the meeting were communicated.

Through those initial conversations generated by the Pizza Experiment, the group began to appreciate that multiple realities often can and do exist—that everyone brings their perspective, their interpretation of values, and their understanding of communications to an issue. We also began to appreciate the importance of all perspectives in our ecosystem before we begin to pass judgment.

The group's honesty conversations centered on transparency, openness, and access to information. Individuals around the table had different expectations of transparency, which became the lens through which they judged a person's relative honesty. For example, the omission of information not relative to one's position may be acceptable to some, but the lack of transparency was deemed dishonest by others. The group also began to appreciate that opinions, perspectives, or absence of facts can easily be interpreted as misrepresentations or dishonesty.

I realized that the notion of transparency can be a huge challenge for leaders. As a CPA, I was taught the importance of confidentiality as a fundamental responsibility of the profession. I learned to protect information—to be guarded in my communications. Andesa's client contracts contain provisions regarding confidentiality, and employees are expected to execute confidentiality agreements. Many security policies and practices are modeled on the need-to-know principle: access to information must be necessary for the individual's job role and function. We have become accustomed to nondisclosure agreements before we even begin a conversation with a prospective client. How does an organization and its leaders meet these confidentiality and nondisclosure demands while balancing the demand for transparency?

Leaders must deal with ambiguity in business every day yet are expected to be transparent about what they do know—even though it is the rare occasion where all facts are available to us. Decisions must often be made based mainly on opinion and perceptions—with your gut, if you will. The idea that you might be called out for dishonesty because you've made a decision in error, lacking access to all the salient facts, presents a high bar.

I began to grasp the nuances in communicating the why and the how of the decision, and why it was necessary to share whatever data there was, as well as its interpretation. When opinions came into play in decision-making, it was important for others to know that they were based on the best data we had, and that as more information was learned, the decision would be reevaluated and potentially reconsidered.

The conversations with my colleagues challenged me to reflect. Am I being honest if I choose not to share everything? As one who leads as a learner, I default to providing information as the best way to educate and create common perspective. I value collaboration as a problem-solving style, so openness, gathering of facts, multiple perspectives, and dialogue about a topic or issue is my preferred style.

Sometimes, values come into conflict: when does honesty trump respect, for instance. What emerged from the deliberations of our participants was that a broad interpretation of honesty may violate other values, such as respect and responsibility. Ultimately, we agreed that we should strive for open and honest communication but not at the expense of violating other values. The objective of an honest environment is the betterment of the individual and the organization. Mutual respect, mutual trust, and strong relationships flourish in the sunlight provided by a transparent environment.

What Does Honesty Look Like?

What honesty looks like at Andesa is a commitment to keeping our communications as open, genuine, transparent, and accurate as possible, always mindful of the ultimate intent of improving a relationship, individual, situation, or the organization. The more we value honesty, the better we see it as an essential building block to upholding long-term relationships.

> The more we value honesty, the better we see it as an essential building block to upholding long-term relationships.

The group also identified those times where being honest can be most challenging. When there is fear of retribution or retaliation or a potential negative financial impact, we need to be cognizant of our value of honesty. How we handle confidential information and how we honor that trust in our communications requires a reflection on honesty.

What do leadership behaviors look like when they model honesty? First, those behaviors place an emphasis on relationships. Honest communication creates a bond of trust, one that allays suspicions of a hidden agenda. One-on-one sessions become a safe place where everything is out in the open and there is freedom to communicate without fear of repercussions.

Second, an honest leader is focused on the coaching and development of those they serve. They are familiar with each team member's strengths and opportunities for improvement. An honest leader is open and candid about growth opportunities and supports the employee's efforts to take advantage of those opportunities.

In addition, an honest leader should be well informed and know where the company is and where it is headed. At a minimum, if the leader doesn't know or can't answer an employee's question, they should be honest and indicate as much, commit to finding the answer, then circle back to complete the communication. Many leaders struggle with the ambiguity inherent in leadership, as if somehow not knowing everything makes them appear less credible. In fact, an answer of "I don't know—but let me find out" inspires trust.

Honesty in Client Relationships

Honesty is pervasive in our industry. What do client relationships and communications look like when honesty is modeled? When I think of values-based leaders in the insurance industry, the first name that comes to mind is Lincoln Financial Group's VP of executive benefits and term strategic operations, Emma Ladd. I asked Emma to share her reflection on the importance of honesty in our industry.

VOICES OF THE INDUSTRY
HONESTY

Honesty is personal. It is more than telling the truth—it is about seeking truth, being real, and caring for others. Honesty is a characteristic that, for me, started taking shape during childhood by watching my role models—my parents—interact. Listening to their daily conversations around the dinner table and seeing the genuine care they showed to family, friends, and coworkers taught me the importance of cultivating meaningful relationships with honesty as the cornerstone value.

Professionally, honesty is a critical part of relationship building and problem-solving. In 2004, I had an experience with Andesa leadership that laid the groundwork for a strong partnership. As a newly appointed head of operations, I met with former executives at Andesa to discuss service-level expectations, because Andesa was not meeting the mark. Simply put, deadlines were missed, and products were flawed. My charge was to either fix this situation with Andesa or look for another partner. While the latter option may have appeared easier to pursue, instead I chose to share this feedback directly with Andesa. In the spirit of partnership, I also invited Andesa to share their perspective about Lincoln's processes and procedures—what could we be doing better to make the relationship successful? We determined that there were inconsistencies within Lincoln that contributed to the missed deadlines and product mistakes. Collaboratively, Andesa and Lincoln established new processes and procedures to ensure business delivery. We developed cultural norms built around open, honest, and direct communication.

Honesty cuts through the red tape to solve a problem. It exposes strengths and weaknesses and invites all parties in a relationship to take accountability for their actions.

Like all things, there is a balanced approach when providing honest feedback—the goal is not to hurt the other party; rather, it is to seek truth together.

I can always proudly reflect on my years with Lincoln, knowing that the core values of the company's namesake align with mine. In voice and example, Abraham Lincoln valued honesty and doing what is right.

Personally and professionally, honesty in action has enabled me to lead with authenticity and care for others.

Andesa's experience indicates clients want open, honest conversations—even if it is a difficult message they might not want to hear. In return, the client respects our communications and perspectives, and trust grows through the interchange. Sometimes, being honest in addressing the client's requests and needs means that we direct the client to what they really need, despite the potential result of less revenue for Andesa. That might hurt us in the short term, but the client will respect and trust Andesa more in the long run. Honesty builds trust and contributes to long-term success.

Many of Andesa's systems have been built through cocreation or collaboration with our clients. This often leads to the creation of a valuable new tool or product supported by Andesa. Once, an opportunity offered by a newer client put our honesty to the test. If we were successful in winning the business, we would have expanded our capabilities in a direction in which we were eager to go. Through the "request for proposal" process with the client, it became apparent that while we believed we could build a successful solution given enough time, we did not think we could deliver in the time frame the client required. After some serious internal discussions, we shared our perspective with the client and withdrew from consideration of that opportunity. Subsequently, we have implemented multiple successful projects with that client, and our business has grown over the years as a result. But what is more interesting to me is that when serving as a reference for Andesa, this particular client always mentions our honesty in withdrawing from the proposal process, rather than our successful projects, as the defining moment in our relationship.

The Andesa examination of the value of honesty provides the evidence of which Jefferson speaks—that wisdom grows with time and suffering, and that honesty is the first chapter in the book of wisdom.

TO SUCCEED:

- Leaders must create and maintain a safe environment, and that begins with honesty.
- Honest leaders make good leaders. Leaders should be comfortable sharing thoughts and feelings in addition to facts.
- Honesty is hard work and may require a price. It leads to authenticity and transparency, builds relationships, and creates a virtuous environment.

KEY QUESTIONS FOR REFLECTION:

- Can we afford NOT to be honest?
- Is honesty an absolute value or just relative?
- If you were totally and consistently honest, what would change?

CHAPTER SEVEN

Initiative

Taking initiative is a form of self-empowerment.
—Stephen Covey

By January of 2017, Andesa had begun to hit its stride on its five-year 2015 strategic plan. Several business development successes had us moving into new product markets. A team was working on a redesign of our systems to improve the user experience. The entire staff was busy learning, implementing, and executing our strategic goals.

Senior System Architect Donovan Rego walked into the senior team meeting that January to present a white paper on the core policy administration engine software for which he was responsible. Two years from retirement, when it would have been easy to settle into the status quo and ride off into the sunset, Donovan instead acknowledged that this core application needed significant investment to withstand future market challenges and have an evergreen future. His analysis was factual, thorough, and compelling. The data supported his conclusions and recommendations. The approach would fundamentally shift the system, which had been developed largely in reaction to our clients' needs, to a much more proactive, architectural design. The challenge for Andesa was the estimated project effort would take five to seven man-years—and that time had not been budgeted. Some other strategic initiatives would need to be deferred to muster the resources necessary to address this situation—and that's exactly what we did.

As we conducted our values focus group conversations, Donovan's example of initiative was a fresh story and most often cited by the development staff in the group. For me, it underlined the truth that a single employee-owner who takes the initiative, invests the time, and provides solutions can change the course of the organization in a significant way. Stephen Covey said it best: "I am personally convinced that one person can be a change catalyst, a 'transformer' in any situation, any organization. Such an individual is yeast that can leaven an entire loaf. It requires vision, initiative, patience, respect, persistence, courage, and faith to be a transforming leader."[15]

In fact, Donovan's recommendation shifted the strategic technology investment at Andesa for several years. While he contributed significantly toward several technology projects and client successes, this demonstration of initiative (and responsibility) took him to another level in the eyes of his colleagues.

One key outcome of the initiative value conversations was the creation of an initiative program, a sort of electronic suggestion box and precursor to Andesa's overall continuous quality-improvement program, launched a few years later. Arthur Parisi, Stephanie Corby, and Anthony Orlando took the first steps in the design and nurture of

---

15   Stephen R. Covey, *Principle-Centered Leadership* (New York: Fireside, 1992), 287.

the Initiative Program efforts. They ensured the quality of Donovan's approach (problem identification, supporting data, recommendation and implementation plan) made its way into the Initiative Program process. This program reinforced the value of initiative by inspiring the submitter to identify an issue, demonstrate the commitment to the research, and plan for resolution, along with responsibility for follow-through. Imagine how the process helps improve the skillsets of those who demonstrate the initiative to proceed with a submission! Imagine how embracing the Initiative Program experience helps someone along the path to realizing their full potential. Not every initiative submitted is approved—but in the few short years since launch, over eighty-seven initiatives have been submitted for review, with thirteen enhancements fully implemented and an additional forty-seven at some stage of implementation. While many of these focus on application efficiencies, many also are submitted to enhance the overall employee experience.

When Donovan retired in 2019 after seventeen years of service, the Initiative Program honored him by creating an annual award presented to an employee who demonstrates the value of initiative. Hallie Langley was recognized as the first recipient of "the Donovan." While working on a client implementation project, she noted that a third-party tool embedded in our software was causing issues that resulted in excess hours, missed estimates, and, perhaps most importantly, negatively impacted developer morale. Hallie's efforts upgraded the tool to the latest version, automated some data source integration, incorporated some fundamental best practices for the application, and significantly improved the documentation for the development team. Her efforts saved Andesa (and our clients as a result) hundreds of hours of effort, eliminated application failures, and improved the ability to support the application in the future.

Initiative Can Be Learned—
If We Take the Initiative

I recently celebrated Compliance Specialist Dan Fowler's first year with the firm. One year into an employee's tenure at Andesa, I check in with that person over an anniversary lunch. It provides me the opportunity to catch up and ensure their Andesa experience is what they envisioned when they joined the Andesa family. Dan shared how he had created a spreadsheet that he completes at the end of each day. One column tracks the situations where he demonstrated initiative and the other notes when he could have or perhaps should have but didn't. It is his tool for self-reflection and has become a model for leaning into a value with which he has struggled but hopes to fully embrace.

One of Dan's celebrated moments during his first year was the submission and approval of an idea through the Initiative Program: the creation of the John Walker Award, which each year recognizes an employee who exemplifies the values and personifies the relentless pursuit of the Andesa Forever Vision in their personal growth, enables others to achieve their full potential, offers the ultimate in client satisfaction/value, and promotes an engaged employee-owner culture. Driven by a desire to "create additional positivity about Andesa," Dan successfully navigated the concept through the Initiative Program. His personal growth was evident to me, and his professional confidence had blossomed during his time with our firm.

Andesa's purpose is to create an environment that encourages and facilitates our employee-owners to develop and apply their business skills to the fullest so both our clients and employee-owners can achieve their full potential. Each step along the way contributes to this environment. Donovan's initiative inspired others to create the Initiative Program. Arthur, Stephanie, and Anthony's leadership and initiative encouraged Hallie to submit and implement her ideas, resulting in her recognition as the first Donovan Award recipient. Dan's reflection led him to step forward and create a broader recognition of the importance of our values. These examples show that initiative isn't limited to any generation or tied to the length of a person's tenure. Whether nearing retirement after decades with Andesa or launching their career from college with less than a year of service, they chose to seize initiative and make an impact in the Andesa ecosystem. All six individuals benefited the company and ecosystem at some level but also grew in confidence and influence because of their willingness to embrace and invest in initiative.

Initiative Grows the Individual

Whether we're talking about an individual, a team, or an organization, the absence of initiative leads to stagnation and irrelevance—sort of a passionless existence. John Walker connects the importance of this value to Andesa's purpose of helping individuals and clients realize their full potential:

> *Initiative is valued in an ethical environment. It encourages people to live up to their potential. And while it is good for an organization when its people excel, it is equally beneficial to the individual. Personal growth and satisfaction are common results of a job well done. In an environment that rewards hard work, initiative, and willingness to accept responsibility, management will seldom need to correct for shirking or failure to do one's job.*[16]

I recently had another anniversary lunch with a teammate who had seemed shy and somewhat intimidated when she'd first met the

---

16   John Walker, *Value from Values: The Making of Andesa Services.*

CEO as she began her career with Andesa. One year later, she led the luncheon discussion and explained what she had learned and accomplished, as well as how she now trains our new hires. When we challenge someone to achieve their full potential, it is so much more than just their role in the company that is improved.

> Whether we're talking about an individual, a team, or an organization, the absence of initiative leads to stagnation and irrelevance—sort of a passionless existence.

It is no secret that the culture of an organization is a critical element in the determination of its long-term success. At Andesa, we use the terms "team" and "family" interchangeably to describe our culture. After reflection on an email that welcomed a new **teammate** to the Andesa **family**, I asked the values focus group about the meanings and emotions behind each term as it applies in a business context. Which term did they prefer to define their time at Andesa? The group's preferences were evenly split.

Many identified primarily with the "team" concept, because we are a group of individuals assembled by talents and attributes to achieve a common goal. *Cooperative, professional,* and *collaborative* are words used to describe the interaction. Teams are about the goals, the numbers, and the results. Teams need to be led. Great teammates place the team first and hold each other accountable. They set high standards and expectations and give maximum effort to achieve the objective. When the conversation is about the business and business growth (i.e., about a particular project that requires us to work together to accomplish a common goal or change the status quo), I try to emphasize the "Andesa team" in my communications.

Those staff members who preferred the "family" metaphor focused on relationships, using words that stressed the human connection, such as *understanding*, *supportive*, *safe*, *open*, *caring*, and *unity* to describe their interactions. At this level, there is no separation between the personal commitment and the business. It's not about win-lose but about commitment to each other and the journey. It's probably not surprising that championship-caliber teams often achieve such a high level of emotional engagement that the players feel they are part of a family.

Families are about people and relationships. *Educate*, *mentor*, and *encourage* are the words that come to mind when we use family as a business descriptor. My wife, Katherine, and I love our children. We encourage them to be independent, to strive for their best, to not settle, and to reach their full potential. It is out of a spirit of love and caring that we encourage and support them. When the desire is to create a caring, supportive, mentoring atmosphere at Andesa or when the emphasis is on relationships and personal growth, I try to emphasize the "Andesa family" in my communications.

Andesa's goals are to have a great employee environment, highly satisfied clients, and a financially successful and sustainable business for the long term. These goals require us to perform as a team to consistently meet interim objectives and, equally important, to behave as a family, being personally committed to one another because we are all in this together. Finding the proper balance between team and family is critical. At minimum, our expectations are that each of us buy into the vision, live the values of the organization, hold each other accountable, and support each other through the ups and downs.

From our values work, I began to see how our first four values (respect, integrity, courage, and honesty) aligned more as family values—focused on relationships and how we were going to behave toward one another and those in our ecosystem. I also understood how initiative and responsibility seemed more team based—the results of the family-based culture we had created and the behaviors that lead to the business results of the firm.

Initiative spurs action. It is the small voice within that urges us to put our thoughts into motion, to activate, to take that step away from what is toward the possibilities of what might be. Fear, uncertainty, and comfort with the status quo are the natural enemies of initiative. For some of us, initiative requires us to muster the courage to act. For others, it speeds the momentum toward improvement and achievement.

Our focus group conversations contrasted the proactive mindset of an innovative culture with the structure and process that accompanies an efficiency-driven environment. Both innovation and efficiency are hallmarks of a successful business, and they are not mutually exclusive. The key is for the individual, team, department, and organization to understand where it is appropriate to be creative and take initiative and where it is better to be more cautious.

Overcoming the Stasis of the Status Quo

Stephen Covey notes, "Employers and business leaders need people who can think for themselves—who can take initiative and be the solution to problems."[17] Thus, initiative is not just identifying a problem. In an ownership culture, talking about a problem but doing nothing to resolve it is just complaining. Initiative spurs us to take the next step toward finding a workable solution. Initiative pushes us

---

17   Stephen R. Covey, "Our Children and the Crisis in Education," *HuffPost*, June 20, 2010, https://www.huffpost.com/entry/our-children-and-the-cris_b_545034.

to seek deeper understanding of an issue, to analyze the observations and data, to reframe our thinking.

Initiative is such a critical value in an ownership culture, because the stasis of the status quo is such a huge force. Commitment and determination are required for any initiative to overcome the politics, turf, competing priorities, potential criticism, and fear. Initiative at Andesa demands that the individual not only start the ignition but drive the bus to its intended destination. Well-intentioned initiatives can easily be brought to a grinding standstill unless passion and per-severance are also present.

We often think about innovation as some larger-than-life break-through that changes the world. However, most improvement initia-tives are small personal developments that make life a little easier. Look around our offices and you'll see a lot of whiteboards, often with a group of employees standing before them brainstorming ideas and jointly trying to figure out solutions. What impresses me most about our business analysts and developers is their desire to not just solve the problem but to do so in a manner that is sustainable and supportable for others on the team. These solutions often save others time, improve accuracy, and enhance our service response time for the long term.

Initiative and Leadership

What do leadership behaviors look like when they model initiative? A critical role for the values-based leader at Andesa is to create an envi-ronment that encourages intrinsic motivation—a culture that inspires rather than stymies initiative. Two words come to mind when reflect-ing on leaders who encourage initiative—humility and patience.

Humility means that leaders must check their ego at the door for the benefit of the team. Most decisions we make aren't actually binary:

they can have multiple right paths forward and do not always rise to the level of "bet the company" status. The leader who recognizes this can challenge the team to embrace the opportunity to learn. As Mark Twain wisely said, "Good decisions come from experience. Experience comes from making bad decisions." Encouraging initiative often means demonstrating the humility to support a decision or direction even when the leader suspects it's not the best choice for the long-term benefit of the team's development.

Stimulating initiative requires another virtue from leadership: patience. Many leaders rise to positions of influence thanks to their technical expertise. Their business acumen places them in a role in which the issues of the day are often brought to their attention—often with the team seeking direction or a solution. The natural inclination of the leader is toward action: provide answers, offer solutions, or perhaps play the role of hero-rescuer and intervene to resolve the problem. Don't do it!

Most day-to-day issues can and should be handled by the team. It is often easier for the leader to simply do or give directions than to take the time to coach, challenge, and mentor. But when a leader takes ownership of a task, it limits the opportunity for the employee to seize initiative and assume responsibility. This is when patience can be a virtue, and an astute leader will lead with questions, not answers. This allows the staff member to resolve the situation, spurring their personal growth. The leader who cultivates initiative navigates this delicate balance of doing versus encouraging others to

> The leader who cultivates initiative navigates this delicate balance of doing versus encouraging others to do for themselves.

do for themselves, and it can make all the difference in the creation of a motivated team equipped to sustain an operation for the long term.

Fostering a collaborative environment allows individuals to share experiences, provides insight into what works and what doesn't, and makes room for people to grow and improve. Understanding where each employee-owner is in terms of their own development, confidence, and capacity permits the leader to provide rightsized opportunities to explore and experiment. Granted, any time you provide an employee or a team a growth opportunity, you are trading off timeliness. And yet, also appreciate that you cannot grow the talent in the organization without providing the opportunity for these types of opportunities to be embraced.

But be careful: a leader can block an initiative mindset without even realizing it. A micromanager who operates from a command-and-control approach produces an environment in which creativity and collaboration are stifled. Many businesses are knowledge based, yet we design the workplace to model a repetitive, task-based production line. Bureaucracy and "process for process's sake" result from leaders who believe they create value through standards and controls, yet in doing so foster a work environment devoid of ingenuity, inventiveness, and responsibility. My own "brilliant ideas" early in my career were often met by leaders with typical enthusiasm-zappers like, "That's not how we do that here" or "We tried that once, and it was a disaster" or, my favorite, "They will never go for it." Who is "they"? Don't "they" include you and me?

Many leaders squelch the energy for initiative by their words and actions. I must confess that I often engage a teammate in some conversation about an idea, and the first words out of my mouth are something cynical; humor was (and still is) my natural defense mechanism. I hope I would never say something like "that's a dumb idea," but my sarcasm can have the same impact as if I had shouted those exact words. I was not even aware of how my behaviors annihilated the passion and energy from my colleagues. While they expected me to jump into the task alongside them, my initial reaction had the opposite effect in the moment and inhibited initiative among the team over the long term.

I believe Dan Pink, in his bestseller *Drive*, provides terrific insight for leaders who desire to create a culture where self-motivation, and thus initiative, can incubate:

A. Lead with questions, not answers.

B. Engage in dialogue and debate, not coercion.

C. Conduct autopsies without blame.

D. Build red flag mechanisms. In other words, make it easy for employees and customers to speak up when they identify a problem.[18]

Imagine how much more effective my leadership would have been if I held my sarcastic tongue and followed this counsel. My colleagues were looking for support. If instead I had sought to understand and challenge the idea, seeking a different perspective or better solution or provided some encouragement, what might have been the possible outcome? I'd like to think I've learned my lessons, but I am sure I still have those moments when I fall back into my initiative-zapping ways.

How does initiative play out across the insurance ecosystem? One of Andesa's long-standing clients with aligned values articulated it the following way.

---

18 Daniel Pink, *Drive: The Surprising Truth about What Motivates Us* (New York: Riverhead Books, 2009).

VOICES OF THE INDUSTRY
INITIATIVE

Initiative comes in all forms, trivial and sizable, and can be driven by one individual or a push by many. As a leader you may be the one proposing a plan that directly affects your unit or inspiring your team to support a broader strategy that is directed at the enterprise level. However, when employees take ownership of solving a problem or proposing new ideas and follow through on those concepts, it results in a team that feels valued and more engaged. It empowers employees to contribute and take leadership while fueling growth for the future.

Taking the initiative to seize opportunities helped propel my career and benefited my company simultaneously. My relentless pursuit of process improvements, automation, risk mitigating controls, and cross training has not only been rewarding but helped lay the groundwork for others to emulate. I have come to realize how much my drive to take action without direction motivates me and has contributed to my success. However, I learned that managing a team does not require that I have all the answers. In order for my team to succeed and develop their own skills, I needed to step back so they could step up. It exemplifies the culture we strive for, which encourages employees to participate and lead change. It also gives employees a sense of ownership in what they do. Employees who have the mindset and support to challenge the status quo become more valuable assets to the company. It will prompt efficiencies and drive positive and continuous improvements, creating a competitive edge.

In our specialized business, we have seen grassroots initiatives that have gained significant traction as a result of the industry striving for a positive and collective outcome. The initiatives of life insurance associations, brokers, and carriers have helped protect products from having an unfavorable result from potential regulatory changes. Lobbying, communication, and perseverance have allowed political contacts to stay informed and understand the ramifications of certain proposals that may negatively affect the industry. In these examples, it is the initiative of a few that energizes others to support the greater good of the COLI/BOLI industry and its clients.

Taking initiative has played an important role in my personal growth, the growth of my company, and the growth of our industry. I have observed how it has been equally important to our friends and colleagues at Andesa Services. They are enthusiastic about living their core values through the work they perform each day and are especially passionate about ensuring their employees live and breathe that mindset. It is through our partnership that I have continued to witness how Andesa's initiative and collaborative approach to new challenges have contributed to our mutual success.

Initiative can incubate from any point within the ecosystem. Often, ideas germinate from Andesa employee-owners who monitor industry developments such as application security, data protection, or third-party solution upgrades. This sense of employee ownership is self-actualized in action. Identifying and solving client issues before the client is aware is the hallmark of any innovative company. Donovan's initiative to revitalize the core engine for future sustainability mentioned earlier is an example of this internal initiative benefiting the whole.

I've often sat in sessions where sales prospect feedback or client security audit questionnaires have led to Andesa initiating enhancements. These actions are necessary to ensure the system can remain vibrant and evergreen, part of caring, feeding, and nurturing of the Andesa ecosystem.

Other examples are market- or client-led initiatives that are incorporated to benefit the entire ecosystem. I spoke earlier in this book about our client cocreation model of innovation: a recent example of a market-led proposal was a request by several brokers to allow for single reporting across Andesa's ecosystem. An insurance broker is often licensed to sell products from multiple insurance carriers. While there is a single Andesa system, each insurance company client (carrier) has unique products, attributes, and requirements. The flexibility and configurability of the Andesa application is a key differentiator in providing service to this market. The underlying data is owned by the carrier and is logically separated in databases within the applications. To create a single report or file feed required us to concatenate (i.e., to link) information from several sources to allow for "all carrier" reporting. That saved the broker's staff time and minimized possible errors by eliminating the need to run individual carrier reports and upload into other solutions for manual editing.

Our Bro-Cat project team (short for Broker Concatenation) first solicited support, funding, and approval from our carriers. No one carrier was asked to fully fund the project. Andesa was willing to invest in the enhancement of the overall ecosystem, and carriers were willing to share in a portion of the cost of the solution to benefit the whole. The team further understood that there would be other brokers who would have their own unique reporting requirements, so it was imperative to construct this solution in a way that would allow for future configurations.

The continuous quality-improvement mindset expected by our employees, clients, and yes, even the marketplace starts with the voice of the client. Improvements to our systems and services make us better and provide better value and impact for our clients. Our overall purpose calls us to help our employee-owners and our clients reach their full potential. This proactive investment in relationships creates the opportunity to identify trends, issues, and opportunities through collaborative feedback and results in a stronger and more sustainable ecosystem.

I've reflected a lot on Stephen Covey's quotes on initiative in writing this chapter. I'll share one more: "Being proactive is more than taking initiative. It is recognizing that we are responsible for our own choices and have the freedom to choose based on principles and values rather than on moods or condition. Proactive people are agents of change and choose not to be victims, to be reactive, or to blame others."[19] Now, let's look at responsibility as a value.

TO SUCCEED:

- Initiative is about action. It creates the momentum toward improvement and achievement.
- Leaders should intentionally stress performing as a team and behaving as a family in communications.
- Initiative can incubate from anywhere and anyone in the ecosystem for the long-term benefit of the individual, team, organization, or ecosystem (sometimes all four).

---

19 Stephen R. Covey, *The 8th Habit: From Effectiveness to Greatness* (New York: Simon and Schuster, 2013), 152.

KEY QUESTIONS FOR REFLECTION:

- How do we balance control over task management and employee initiative? Between efficiency and innovation?
- When was the last time you helped someone achieve their goals?
- Do you trust your teammates enough to allow them to seize the initiative?
- Is your motivation self-interest based (prove my point) or improvement-based?

CHAPTER EIGHT

Responsibility

Leaders are not responsible for the results, leaders are responsible for the people who are responsible for the results.
—**Simon Sinek,** *The Infinite Game*

It's said that in every life, some rain must fall—but the storm of disruption brought on by COVID-19 has been more like a tsunami, and as of this writing, we're still in the midst of it. What do leaders do when an event like this appears on the horizon? They take responsibility—and prepare.

We were enjoying the short-lived celebrations of our transition from a minority-owned ESOP to 100 percent employee-owned when Andesa felt the first impacts of COVID-19. It was Steve Budihas, Andesa's senior executive responsible for policy administrative services, who suggested in a February team meeting that, given the increasingly alarming news, we should revisit our preparedness plan. Our crisis management team was asked to review it and report back with recommendations for Andesa and its employee-owners.

Our first concern was risk management. We couldn't control the spread of the virus, but we could control how ready we were to serve our clients, conduct our business, and, most importantly, protect our employees and their families. Laura Fell and Beth Kulig from human resources, along with Chip Whiteside and Ryan Scanlan from the risk-management office, joined forces to form our pandemic response team (or PRT for short). They were tasked with monitoring the situation for new developments, providing advice, and managing internal corporate communications. In a world full of ever-evolving information and expectations, this team provided steadfast energy and guidance through a most challenging time.

The PRT coordinated daily stand-up meetings with the senior leadership, IT operations, and legal to update and advise on policy decisions. Andesa had a goal to shift more than 50 percent of its workforce to a remote environment. We initially expected to operate on a short-term rotation approach, whereby staff would switch in and out of the office every couple of weeks. Within the first two weeks of our implementation, 75 percent of our operating work force was working virtually. As the virus situation deteriorated in the areas where our offices were located, the PRT recommended a complete office shutdown. The day after Pennsylvania's governor closed non-life-sustaining businesses unless they were able to telework, we completed the transition to 100 percent work from home.

The 180 employee-owners of Andesa understood their business responsibilities and displayed the resourcefulness and resiliency to adjust to the new environment. PRT's daily stand-up meetings coordinated operating issue resolutions like network bandwidth, mail forwarding, remote call forwarding, security enhancements, individual employee equipment needs, scheduled deliveries, and communications to clients. Communications across Andesa were frequent. As higher order needs were addressed, the PRT shifted its focus to the communication of additional safety and wellness information as well as plans for a longer-than-expected virtual office environment.

While the company adjusted to our new work environment, client relationship managers maintained close contact with our client partners to better understand their challenges. We needed to ensure that adequate service and coverage were available across the ecosystem and that our work was aligned with our clients' needs and changing expectations.

PRT conducted random pulse surveys of employees during the initial weeks of the crisis. Feedback was incorporated into the company's plans and served to improve the communications to the entire company. As weeks turned into months and working from home became the new normal, Andesa's employees were engaged as if they were in the office: supporting one another, serving our clients, delivering on project commitments, and advancing our technology.

A team led by our CFO, Mark Wilkin, constructed a pandemic resource hub on our intranet. The site served as a central clearing house of credible COVID-19 information for our teams. This single source of company communications and work-from-home policies also linked to trustworthy sources for information about the disease, healthcare, mental health resources, federal policies, and benefit changes. Information on our benefit plans, student loans, tax relief, and links to community resources and recommended online personal finance courses were provided. Realizing that some of our teammates might suffer financial hardship due to spouses being furloughed from their jobs, the PRT team created an accelerated hardship loan application and review process. The team also recommended a small stipend to all employees to help improve their home office environments as remote work turned from weeks to months.

It was an all-hands-on-deck situation. Across Andesa, employee-owners collaborated to make a difference and preserve our culture. What we valued in the office now needed to be replicated across a virtual environment. Examples of employee-owned and employee-led admirable behavior included the following:

- Leaders on the operations team developed a model to onboard new hires in a 100 percent remote environment. The program was designed to build relationships and communicate expectations to new hires before their transition to full-time work from home. This comprehensive approach engaged leadership and staff from across the organization to make an important first impression and impact.

- Virtual team happy hours and periodic company-wide virtual gatherings were established to provide everyone an opportunity to touch base. Many stayed connected to one another after hours through the online gaming community.

- Our Employee Activities Team (EAT) conducted a virtual "take your child to work" experience. To encourage a healthy lifestyle, EAT extended our normal summer wellness event, where participants reported their activity minutes and often filmed themselves performing challenges for extra team points. Though we missed the camaraderie of group events such as kickball, office walks, and mini golf outings, over half the company participated in "Andesa on the Move"!

Our final survey that summer revealed that 99 percent of our employees believed we acted and communicated with clarity, 91 percent felt supported by their managers, 88 percent said they were connected to their teams, and 87 percent indicated they had everything they needed to work from home effectively.

Values-based employee-owners seize the initiative to deliver quality results for their team, their teammates, their company, their clients, and the broader ecosystem. My fellow employee-owners embraced their responsibility and demonstrated tireless agility, dedication, and problem-solving abilities. Thanks to their efforts, Andesa remained operationally solid and highly productive during a period of severe disruption.

> Values-based employee-owners seize the initiative to deliver quality results for their team, their teammates, their company, their clients, and the broader ecosystem.

Responsibility in Focus

John Walker connects the importance of responsibility to Andesa's purpose of creating an environment in which individuals and clients can pursue their full potential:

> *In addition to providing opportunity, growth, and decent treatment, an ethical environment promotes a sense of responsibility in its employees. An employee who is treated well by his firm is likely, in return, to take ownership of the work he does and care about the well-being of the firm. Industriousness is often a by-product of a culture where hard work is expected and rewarded. A willingness to work hard for the firm's success translates into a team mentality that inspires employees to sacrifice time, emotion, and effort when the good of the firm requires it.*[20]

20　John Walker, *Value from Values: The Making of Andesa Services.*

Was I surprised by the Andesa response to COVID-19? No! That's how we roll. It's not task-based ownership or economic ownership that we value. It is a higher sense of emotional connection to the company—a personal responsibility—a true ownership mentality. Anytime you accept a task, you accept responsibility. Andesa's employee-owners understand their role, their responsibilities, and what is expected of them. But they also understand the company's vision, values, goals, aspirations, and expectations. We spend some time each quarter sharing our purpose, what the company is trying to build, and our plan and strategies. We stress the importance of building relationships with our clients and with each other. We lay out the work and, then we support the environment. I'd like to tell you there is some magic "secret sauce" helping the team get to some nirvana state of responsibility. However, it is simply a combination of values, communication, and a positive, respectful environment. The result is a team of people who are willing to sacrifice personally for the good of the whole.

Linda Ellison was the first employee John Walker hired at Andesa Services. When John was writing his book, his editor met with a number of Andesa employees. LE, as Linda is affectionately known, was among those interviewed. Notice that she reflected on how one value—respect—contributes to another value—responsibility. "Respect is another important part of Andesa's environment. By trusting employees, giving them flexibility, Andesa makes them feel a sense of ownership, *responsibility* for the company. The environment induces a passion in its people to make the company work." Her comment from that interview was captured long before Andesa became employee-owned. Respect and responsibility have been embedded into our operating philosophy from the beginning, and those values were evident during the pandemic crisis.

As our values focus group conversations attempted to define responsibility, words like *dependable*, *committed*, *reliable*, and *diligent* emerged. Mark Floyd, one of Andesa's senior developers, shared, "Responsibility is the ability to respond. Accountability is the ability to provide an account." Those words strike me as profound.

Accountability is what we have when we take responsibility for our own actions, when we bear the consequences of our decision or behaviors and don't try to shift blame for our mistakes to others or the system. One of my pet peeves is when a leader says, "We have to hold them accountable." It seems to me that, by that point, the leader is already behind in their duties. Responsibility is forward thinking; accountability is backward looking. If the leader prepares their team to respond and provides them the ability to respond, and they perform as expected, then rarely must they provide an account in the way we typically think about "holding someone accountable." The leader's first instinct should be to prepare and support the team or the individual in their ability to respond. If the individual or team is responsible, the leader rarely needs to worry about accountability.

A nuance in looking at accountability as the ability to account is understanding that accountability *is* someone's responsibility. As CEO, I am responsible for many requirements and objectives in the organization. One of those responsibilities it to provide an account of the organization's results to our board and our employee-owners as the beneficiaries of the company. I do not expect my board or my shareholders to have to hold me accountable. Likewise, I do not expect a client to hold Andesa accountable. I expect Andesa to take responsibility for its commitments, because the client should never have to point out our shortfalls.

As the values focus groups dove deeper into this "responsibility versus accountability" concept, many began to appreciate how responsibility related to the tasks and goals at hand. Responsibility focused on the skills, tools, talent, and attitude to accomplish the objectives to a successful conclusion. Accountability focused on information sharing, communications, and relationships (i.e., the ability to account). We came to understand ownership culture resulted from a combination of both responsibility and accountability. An owner understands their role, has the ability to carry it out, and provides information as appropriate.

Employee-owners perceived that Andesa had high expectations and a high degree of responsibility among the staff. Justin Hartz, who'd recently joined our organization as a developer, shared this sentiment with the group, "We take care of each other. If there's somebody on our team that isn't responsible, they don't last here very long. If you're letting your teammates down, we don't need management to take care of it. We take care of it on our own."

To some, that quote may sound like a bad line from a mafia movie, though I'm sure Justin didn't mean it that way. I came to appreciate that the way we onboard employees leads to a sense of teamwork, ownership, and camaraderie. Mentoring and hands-on, on-the-job training opportunities create expectations for high performance among teammates. If someone doesn't carry their load and prevents the next person from meeting their deliverables, the values of integrity, respect, courage and honesty kick in. Individuals on the team intervene around expectations and teamwork. Teammates build relationships, which, in turn, build the initiative and responsibility into the culture.

Allow me to share an example: Our development team recently identified third-party software embedded in one of our applications that would no longer be compatible with the latest version of JAVA, the programming language used in many of our systems. This issue would have prevented clients from using Andesa's application, and that was a serious problem. After some initial angst, the team rolled up their sleeves and figured out the best path forward. Development of the replacement software required coordinated testing and collaboration with our client's technology departments. For most of our clients, the change was seamless. Others required detailed understanding of configurations to accept this new method of using the Andesa system within their environment.

As implementation planning progressed, COVID-19 struck. Since we had effectively pivoted to a remote environment, Andesa was ready to launch. However, to prevent undue stress on our clients as they did their own migration to work from home, we chose to delay the implementation. Undeterred, the team partnered directly with our clients to navigate their new environments and coordinated releases so that no client would experience issues. While COVID-19 certainly added some additional steps and elongated the time frame, five or six individuals were able to operate responsibly, without management intervention, with an ownership mindset, and within an ethical, values-based environment, which brought about a perfect resolution.

Taking Responsibility for Team Members' Growth

A key responsibility of leadership in a people-first culture like Andesa is to ensure everyone is provided opportunity for growth toward their full potential. When work opportunities are aligned with an individual's CliftonStrengths talents, the leader creates a framework for positive energy and intrinsic motivation. But we've taken it a step further.

A few years ago, Andesa adopted a model for performance evaluations based on an Entrepreneurial Operating System tool. Labeled the GWC (Get it, Want it, and have the Capacity to *do* it), the conversation between staff and leader begins with a discussion about understanding roles and responsibilities:

Do they …

- **"Get it"** is a conversation comparing expectations from both perspectives, resulting in a clear understanding about the individual "getting" the work.

- **"Want it"** is a conversation about the individual's desire to be in the role they are assigned. Andesa has a high retention rate among its workforce, but for those who do leave, the majority do so because they do not "want it"—the work, that is. There have been several instances where an individual determines they do not want their leadership responsibilities and would prefer being an individual contributor, responsible for tasks and deliverables rather than for people. GWC has allowed us to retain several key and knowledgeable individuals who otherwise would be frustrated in roles they didn't want.

- **"Have the capacity to do it"** is a conversation about skill sets. Here, the leader must provide the needed exposure and opportunity for the individual to improve their competence commensurate with the work required of them. Many capacity conversations result in some additional training or a different assignment to encourage personal growth.

GWC role-clarity conversations also create a framework for understanding a person's responsibilities, willingness, and ability to perform to the expectations as agreed upon.

As it turns out, the majority of GWC conversations are uneventful. Why? The leader and employee-owner are on the same page regarding expectations. There is a desire to fulfill the expectations, and the tools and skills are available to deliver. There are very few performance problems as a result. Responsibility inspires others. Responsibility builds confidence.

I don't mean to suggest that simply encouraging responsibility eliminates the need for accountability and performance management. There will always be competing priorities and uncertainties, which cause mistakes and misunderstandings. But, in my experience, encouraging responsibility and providing the space for someone to create their own sense of ownership taps their intrinsic motivation and usually leads to successful outcomes.

Vince Collier led the broker services division at Andesa for over twenty years. He continues to serve the firm as a board member since his retirement. When he met with John's editor to discuss John's book, he spoke to the importance of nurturing one's intrinsic motivation. At Andesa, he said, "You as an individual are important. As important as the work you do … It's leadership's job to maintain the environment such that it continues to allow people to go where their motivation takes them. This freedom gives employees the opportunity to control their professional growth, to take on responsibility in areas that inspire them. And that is vital to the running of the firm, because motivation has to come from within."

What other leadership behaviors would we expect when a leader models and encourages responsibility? In *Value from Values*, John Walker inspires us at Andesa to lead differently: "Management personnel must themselves be ethical and fully embrace the purpose of the firm. Indeed, unless managers are energized by their efforts to build and maintain the ethical environment, they likely will fail.

Their responsibility is so pervasive that I shudder at the thought of their burden if their work is not a labor of love."[21] The acceptance of the leadership burden John describes produces responsibility for the whole of the organization and the entire ecosystem. Leaders bear the responsibility of surrounding themselves with individuals who share the vision and convictions of the leader and the organization. If it sounds like a tall order, it is. At Andesa, our founder set a standard that is a challenge to meet but a rewarding journey to take.

Any leader who models responsibility will have followers. They create a sense of community, a shared vision, and a trust-based culture. They are not just putting out today's fires; they're assessing the resources and solutions needed for the company to achieve its long-term objectives and sustainability. They help others grow into their full potential. They inspire initiative and generate confidence. Those around them will measure themselves and strive toward the standard modeled. John Walker, Linda Ellison, and Vince Collier serve as stellar role models for a current generation of leaders at Andesa.

Leaders who expect responsibility from their team are themselves responsible and accountable for their team; in other words, they walk the talk. I like to say the leader owns the problems but reflects the successes back to the team and individuals. The objective is continuous, steady improvement over time. Timely and honest feedback is a way to demonstrate to the individual and team you care about them. When a leader creates the sense of a shared vision and clearly communicates goals and expectations, the team will assume responsibility for meeting them, and that collaboration will generate a sense of mutual accountability. People will hold themselves to that standard and be more willing to confront others on the team concerning nonperfor-

---

21   John Walker, *Value from Values: The Making of Andesa Services.*

mance—what Justin, our young developer, was communicating when he said, "We take care of it on our own."

The values focus groups described an ideal leader as coach, consensus builder, communicator, developer, and listener, with a high degree of self-awareness. In an environment where responsibility is nurtured and encouraged, leaders build an environment of trust and psychological safety. Values-based leaders promote a bottom-up leadership approach versus a command-and-control style often associated with micromanagement.

When employee-owners understand what the company is trying to build, its vision, and its values, then leadership can support and serve instead of command and direct. Andesa empowers its employee-owners by giving them the opportunity to step up and share responsibility. Employee teams have been formed over the years to share organizational responsibilities. In addition to the PRT and EAT examples cited earlier, a communications team, a compensation and benefits program review team, numerous implementation project teams, a training team to develop the Andesa Academy, and a diversity and inclusivity team are other examples of this shared-responsibility approach. The Initiative Program mentioned in the previous chapter is employee led. These are examples of employee-owners taking responsibility and owning the outcome. Recently, a team of employees drove the research, selection, adoption, and implementation of our formal continuous quality-improvement program. Their selection of the Kaizen model, with its emphasis on respect for humanity, is perfectly aligned with Andesa's vision and values.

Serving on a team can be hard work. It often requires extra hours and effort, but those who do so find the investment of effort brings its own rewards. This work pushes individuals outside their comfort zone. It gives them an opportunity to work on a different issue, research a unique subject, utilize different talents, and collaborate with others in the organization with whom they normally do not work. They experience autonomy, and they can positively impact their workplace as an individual. This participation contributes to personal growth on their pathway toward their full potential.

It's not an earth-shattering concept: show people respect, treat them with dignity, be transparent about your goals, and put your trust in them, and you will receive respect, initiative, honesty, responsibility, and trust in return. At Andesa, employees feel supported, are encouraged to take risks, and are set up for growth and success.

Growing Your People Is Your Responsibility

As leaders, it's our responsibility to build the individual relationships that allow team members to align with us, their teams, and the company's direction. When a leader is confident, the individual understands their role and has the necessary subject matter expertise—in other words, clarity on the G and C in the GWC conversations—the values of courage, initiative, and responsibility lead us to value the self-motivated individual and challenge them to reach their full potential. Engaging employees in the achievement of their full potential requires active, engaged leadership: intentionally examining the individual, looking beyond the current skills and roles, and helping that person grow beyond what they themselves might have thought possible.

Creating clarity on expectations for individuals as well as for teams is another way to instill responsibility. GWC conversations help at the individual level. At the team level, specificity increases accountability. Another Entrepreneurial Operating System tool, the Vision Traction Organizer, or VTO, is used to communicate our vision, values, goals, strategies, and objectives quarterly across Andesa, to create clarity on an organizational level. We've found that this kind of effective communication encourages buy-in and input into operational and strategic decisions and serves as a basis for responsibility.

> Creating clarity on expectations for individuals as well as for teams is another way to instill responsibility.

Leadership is more art than science, in my opinion. One of my key roles at Andesa is leading a team of leaders to facilitate the collaboration around strategic opportunities and decisions facing the company. As CEO, I create space for talented people to share great ideas and contribute to the company, nurturing their growth personally, professionally, and corporately. I have learned to be more patient, to ask more questions rather than making statements. I bring up different perspectives to challenge the status-quo thinking. Oftentimes, the team or the individual needs to struggle through the problem instead of being rescued by the leader. That is part of their growth journey.

An example of this approach to leadership occurred recently. As Andesa moved through the transition to a 100 percent employee-owned model, it seemed a better approach would be to get more of the organization engaged with the strategic plan that would drive our success for the next five years. It struck me as a much better method than the prior CEO-led, senior-team strategic planning exercise. To that end, we adopted a collaborative strategic planning approach in 2019 with five work areas that involved input from over one-third of the company.

But that was just the beginning. As I looked at my executive team, I had two seasoned leaders and two members newer to their executive responsibilities. The newer members were assigned to serve in their sweet spot and focus on the portion of the plan for their own area. However, the challenge for the two seasoned leaders was different. Those two, the CFO and CIO, were each usually the most knowledgeable person in the room in their respective disciplines. The CFO was given the challenge to develop the plan for the technology area and the CIO was given the challenge to develop the administrative services portion of the operation's team plan. This approach exposed them to different portions of the business. It also challenged them to lead differently. They had to ask questions rather than give answers.

While leadership clarity is important, I incorporated an alternative strategy when working with the executive team on the planning process. Leaders rarely operate in an environment where information, direction, and outcomes are crystal clear. Assignments to my team typically start with a problem statement and a whiteboard. This approach forces the "owner" of the assignment to wrestle with the issue from multiple perspectives and grow their leadership skills along the way. As the planning process unfolded, I wanted to see how my team addressed the problems and through what lenses they peered to do their analysis. I was also interested to see how they would link the work to the purpose of Andesa, to our values, to our strategic plan and objectives. For my part, I tried to guard against my own bias by being curious and open to ideas that might emerge from the process. By repeatedly challenging leaders in this regard, I observed a deeper sense of ownership for the idea and plan.

This collaborative planning model led our leaders to expand their toolbox and establish new relationships with people across the organization. The teams delivered fantastic products for the overall strategic plan. Andesa was able to build its institutional planning muscle consistent with our values, which will sustain Andesa long after my tenure with the company.

Some may ask, Didn't that approach take longer? Yes, but Andesa's long-term outlook allows me to take the time needed to drive responsibility deep into the culture. Many technology companies are "get big fast" environments, funded and built for the flip in three to five years. Andesa's value system and approach is different. We are aligned with our client partners in an ecosystem designed to last over 100 years. Our responsibility is to protect and nurture the environment and continuously innovate and improve such that the promises made when the policy is sold in 2020 will be fulfilled when that claim is paid in 2080 or even later.

What Do Client Relationships and Communications Look Like When Responsibility Is Modeled?

I was introduced to New York Life's Dawn Behrens when she assumed the chief operating officer for institutional life/advanced markets role. Charged with the responsibility of digitally transforming the operations to drive client growth and experience, Dawn's vision is refreshing and engaging. I enjoy our conversations, and she has helped advance my own strategic thinking on the matter, an example of the components of the ecosystem strengthening each other. I asked her to share some perspective on the importance of responsibility in our industry.

VOICES OF THE INDUSTRY:
RESPONSIBILITY

Responsibility in business parlance and practice has recently evolved among the mainstream. Once synonymous with ethics, product/service quality, and ultimately shareholder profits, **responsibility** now more broadly applies to a multitude of stakeholders and outcomes. This is evidenced in the growth of B Corps and discussions about the "triple bottom line."

At New York Life, America's largest mutual life insurer, this multistakeholder approach to responsibility has been engrained in our business mindset and conduct through-out our 175-year history. Mutual insurance companies were created as a means for community members to guarantee support for one another in times of need. In the 1990s, as many insurers went public, New York Life stayed the mutuality course. As a key foundational business strategy, mutuality inspired our culture of long-term **responsibility** to our policy owners, employees, and communities. Mutuality is the constant underlying our corporate strategy and practices. This includes the mindset and conduct of our employees and agents, who serve our policy owners and volunteer in communities where they live and work.

As Ron has shared about Andesa Services, the power of responsibility has been evident every day at New York Life, especially as the pandemic disrupted life in 2020. Our leaders quickly mobilized to shift 95 percent of employees to work at home in a matter of days. With this came trust in and reliance on employees to adapt processes and make appropriate decisions to keep the business running.

Beyond keeping our employees safe and supporting the financial needs of our clients, New York Life realized it could and should do more. Within a matter of weeks, employees helped launch the Brave of Heart Fund, a cofounded endeavor by the New York Life and Cigna Foundations to provide grants to eligible family members of frontline healthcare workers and volunteers who have lost their lives to COVID-19 while caring for others. Once again, our employees embodied and modeled our commitment to responsibility within our communities by mustering energy to deliver this new and impactful fund in addition to addressing other critical business and personal changes the pandemic was bringing on.

We are grateful for our twenty-plus-year partnership with Andesa. The company's employees have a commitment to their stakeholders—clients, including New York Life, Andesa employees as owners, and those within their local communities. These shared corporate values have enabled New York Life and Andesa to successfully work together.

At Andesa, responsible client service requires us to personally own an issue all the way to conclusion—either develop a creative solution or find the right individual who can respond effectively to the matter at hand. That requires effective communication with the client throughout the process.

We understand and appreciate that our clients are striving to accomplish critical objectives. Cooperation and collaboration are necessary to fulfill responsibilities, and priorities have to be aligned if the systems and services are going to operate successfully for the long term. And while both client and Andesa personnel must work together to build a partnership, our relationship managers understand it is their responsibility to make sure that collaboration happens. Consequently, they conduct weekly client meetings to ensure priorities are consistently understood and changes communicated in a timely manner.

Andesa owns the responsibility to maintain the client's core system of record for the long term. We're often challenged to choose between a potential short-term, expedient business solution with a lower initial cost and a more expensive one that may take longer to implement but ultimately will be more sustainable. When a choice like this must be made, it's on us to ask our clients the kinds of questions that give us greater clarity about their business needs and perspectives. As our purpose also includes ensuring our clients achieve their full potential, it is incumbent upon us to understand those expectations. Many times, the solution is found in a quick fix to meet a particular deliverable date, with a longer-term solution being implemented after the initial delivery—giving our client the opportunity to meet their immediate objectives while allowing Andesa to better support the application for the long term.

Since Andesa takes responsibility for the relationships with its clients and employee-owners, it faces a difficult challenge. Those relationships constantly evolve and are in flux. We have discussed how to build an ecosystem, but how do we ensure our values become ingrained and can be maintained and sustained as the ecosystem as the ecosystem grows and evolves? Let's look at the challenges in the next chapter.

TO SUCCEED:

- Leaders build a culture of responsibility in which accountability follows.
- "Get it, want it, and have the capacity to do it" conversations create a culture of responsibility.
- Leaders help others grow and prosper toward their full potential. They inspire initiative and generate confidence.

KEY QUESTIONS FOR REFLECTION:

- Do we know what our duties and responsibilities are? Are we handling them as we should?
- Do we take responsibility as employee-owners? Are we invested in the success of the whole company?
- How does one correct irresponsible behavior when they see it?

CHAPTER NINE

Implementing Values-Based Leadership

You add value to people when you value them.
—**John Maxwell**

The culmination of John Walker's vision for Andesa occurred on January 2, 2020, when the employees of Andesa completed a second-stage ESOP transaction, taking employee ownership in the firm from 8 percent to 100 percent of the company. In addressing the staff via video message, John talked of the early days when the team would sit around and discuss the values of the company. Even then, the vision was that control of the company would remain in the hands of the employees. He shared he was excited we had such a great staff to which to pass on this responsibility. Then he mentioned he was no longer an owner of Andesa and, in John's typical humble manner, noted that he will try his best "to serve the employees as the new owners."

In a similar way, the ESOP transaction was a culmination of my Andesa journey. When I assumed the CEO role nine years earlier, I understood that my success at Andesa was directly related to my ability to steer the organization from its original founders, owners and leaders to a future generation of values-based leaders to continue Andesa on its Forever Vision journey.

The Andesa of today is not the same Andesa that John established in 1983. Our technology and service offerings have expanded. More staff and clients have been added to the ecosystem. Regulatory changes, societal changes, and technology advances contributed to different ways in which we operate, manage risk, and provide value. Yet while the business may be different, our core values and beliefs have remained steadfast. There may have been times over the decades where we failed our values and, perhaps, we haven't always prioritized our purpose. The thirty-sixth-percentile employee-engagement score in 2016 that launched our employee focus group values efforts is Exhibit A in that regard. But the employees' response to this gut punch has built a more purposeful company, which provides an opportunity to continue to pursue our Forever Vision that began decades earlier.

A Purposeful Environment

I am an accountant by training, so the numbers are important to me. But numbers are not the purpose of a business. The major lesson for me through this values-based journey was that the success of our business and the success of our people are inseparably connected. If each of us builds our relationships with each other and our clients with **respect** and **integrity**; if we show the **courage** to venture out of our comfort zones and confront difficult conversations and realities;

if we are transparent, authentic and **honest** with each other; if we demonstrate enthusiasm and seize the **initiative**, and be diligent, **responsible**, and accountable for our choices and our efforts; if we all operate in accordance with our purpose and values day in and day out, then we should be a successful company and contribute value to a healthy and thriving ecosystem.

Author Jon Gordan, in his bestseller *The Carpenter*, challenges us to "love, serve, and care" for each other and each customer.[22] When a leader adopts this "love, serve, and care" values-based approach, they focus on others. My dreams are for others to succeed, to be fulfilled, to rise above levels that they thought possible for themselves.

People are the product in a knowledge-based service business. To imagine that you can effectively lead without truly caring for your team is absurd. Understanding, challenging, loving and supporting our team is my primary responsibility as a leader. Translating this purpose and approach through the organization provides the opportunity for us to create client relationships based on trust and values. As we develop these relationships, we come to understand, challenge, love, and support our client's aspirations and goals. This is critical in our ability to add value and assist in our client's drive to achieve their full potential. Business is about people, and Andesa is in the people business. The entire ecosystem is strengthened when we honor our values and relationships.

To lead a knowledge-based, values-based organization, it is important to think about three activities: build, maintain, and sustain. The remainder of this chapter will focus on stories of navigating the people journey at Andesa.

---

22 Jon Gordon, *The Carpenter: A Story about the Greatest Success Strategies of All* (New Jersey: John Wiley & Sons, 2014).

Build the Team—Recruitment and Promotions

The day I made the transition from CFO to CEO, my peers had become my team. I had gained their support during the prior five years by working alongside them and being a conscientious, supportive, and accountable teammate. I was now managing a group of individuals for whom I had tremendous respect and who had much more experience and industry knowledge than I possessed.

I often hear researcher and author Jim Collins's well-known metaphor "the right people on the bus" used as rationalization for terminations. I like to emphasize the phrase in terms of recruitment and promotions. Your team is a legacy statement for you as their leader. When you hire or promote someone to your team, they bring their values and influence to the organization. Every hiring decision is a reflection on you and the culture you are building—in other words, the rest of the organization and those in the ecosystem are watching. Over the past decade, we have built an impressive leadership team by emphasizing this "right people" principle in the recruitment and promotion of individuals. A leader who seeks to build long-term value considers not only what an individual can contribute at the time of their hire but also whether that individual has the values and makeup to learn and grow as the company and ecosystem grow and evolve. I look for leaders who will carry the torch after my tenure. Let me share the stories of three critical members of my team as examples of how personal growth and challenge benefit the business.

My first hire as CEO was to fill the vacant CFO seat. The CFO role is strategic but also highly tactical. While I prefer to promote from within, there was no accounting team at the time of my transition. Andesa's executive recruiter conducted a national search through which we came to meet Mark Wilkin.

There was an immediate comfort level with Mark. His small-town Pennsylvania background paralleled my own. A big-four public accounting career spoke volumes about his values and work ethic. Andesa had a lot to offer him on his personal growth and life journey, but one concern was whether Andesa could provide him enough challenge over the long term. To create space for his progress, I had to forgo my CFO ways. There was perhaps some personal growth for me in that recognition.

Mark's strengths as an accountant and leader complemented mine. He assumed more and more responsibilities at Andesa. Today, he leads our business development area in addition to his CFO role. I know it sounds strange—sales and finance in one executive. Mark likes to joke that he is "an accountant with a little bit of a personality." I like to think that he is energized through the utilization of his talents to move closer to his full potential. When he was given the opportunity to lead the technology portion of our strategic plan, it was to encourage his leadership growth, and deepen his knowledge of the business. His progress as a communicator, mentor, and values-based leader has been remarkable and a privilege to nurture and encourage.

Andesa's implementation officer, Chris Shalbert, is the embodiment of the Andesa purpose and vision. Chris joined Andesa almost twenty years ago as a client services representative, an entry-level position. While he had prior experience with support and analysis with a local financial planner, Chris threw himself into his responsibilities at Andesa. His tenacity led him to learn the business, Andesa's systems, and the industry while he improved his analytical and design skills. Each step along the way, his responsibilities increased.

Chris became my go-to person when talking to prospects or clients. He was remarkably adept at taking the strategic view, yet able to dive deep into the details of transaction or regulatory processing. He is highly regarded as both a business and technical expert by our clients, but perhaps his greatest growth has come through opportunities to lead people. Exposure to leadership coaching and engagement as part of the senior leadership team has given him a perspective beyond his primary responsibilities.

I was introduced to our lead actuary and director of client experience, Michelle Cramer, by a member of our team who had previously worked with her. His recommendation indicated she was "made for Andesa." I recall leaving our initial lunch meeting with the thought, "I'm not sure where, what, or how I could use her, but we need her." We didn't have an opening—I didn't even have a job description for a lead actuary—but she had tremendous industry experience, and she was a perfect cultural fit. My gut reaction was confirmed when she visited our offices and many on our senior team echoed my assessment.

When Michelle accepted the position, I challenged her to observe the company and then develop a job description where she believed she could add the most value to the firm. Within ninety days, we had a four-pronged plan that focused on supporting clients and building insurance acumen.

Soon after Michelle's arrival, Andesa successfully executed on its strategic plan to expand beyond the COLI and BOLI product lines into more traditional life insurance markets. Michelle was part of the team that headed up this new initiative. Through a challenging implementation project, her ability to collaborate and her leadership skills were evident. Michelle remains a steadfast supporter and champion for the actuarial profession and she readily accepts new internal challenges. Her current role is to lead our client relationship efforts yet still work closely with our actuary developers and business solutions consultants. As we continue to challenge and develop her long-term leadership skills, her next role will further expand her operations leadership responsibilities.

Each member of my team has a similar story of recruitment, challenging assignments, changing roles, continuous learning, and personal growth. But a word of caution when recruiting for values. A leader needs to think of a culture *add* rather than simply a culture *fit* when building a team. Our team is by no means homogenous, and that's what makes us a great team. We share values and a commitment to the purpose and mission, but our talents

> A leader needs to think of a culture *add* rather than simply a culture *fit* when building a team.

and styles both complement and challenge our colleagues. The sum of our parts, the wisdom of the many is stronger than any one of us.

About half the members of Andesa's leadership team were recruited into their roles and about half have been promoted into their position. Historically, we would promote leaders primarily based on technical prowess. But as we experienced our leadership development investment and our values work, today we are promoting more on leadership skills and potential. Whether we hire externally or promote from within, we look for demonstrated leadership experience. Internally, that may be demonstrated in real time on client projects or through leadership of internal teams or task force work. Leadership promotions are less about technical ability and more about the ability to ask questions, organize work, drive to a conclusion or deliverable, get people to collaborate, and help others grow in their roles.

As we recruit at Andesa, we are sensitive to the importance of people to our firm's growth. We think long-term about values, coach-ability, leadership potential, and personal growth. The extension of an offer to an employee is an investment in both our company's and that person's future—it's that important. Through their training, they will learn from and interact with many of the staff. In short order, they will become the teacher and trainer of new hires. And that is where we shift from building the team to maintaining the team.

Maintaining the Team—Mentoring, Training, and Empowerment

Hiring and onboarding are not enough to ensure an individual becomes a long-term, reliable contributor to the organization. Our industry is unique, and our systems are proprietary, so we understand the need to invest in skills development for those who join us. To sustain a knowledge-based, values-based organization, you must ensure an employee's skills are constantly growing. Andesa's purpose of helping our employee-owners reach their full potential aligns with this imperative.

As Andesa emerged from its engagement assessment and values conversations, three primary actions were emphasized. First, we needed to solidify and energize the values throughout the organization. Secondly, we needed an organizational commitment to training and mentoring. Third, we needed to encourage collaboration and empowerment through engagement of the employees.

It was one thing for thirty individuals in the company to deeply examine Andesa's core values, but it would require the translation of that effort into a process where the values were communicated as expected behaviors. It is unrealistic to assume that a company's core values would be understood, interpreted, and applied in each situation identically across 180 employees. The challenge was to ensure that employee behaviors are aligned with the company's values as much as possible.

A small group of the participants in the values focus groups were challenged with the creation of a process by which we would educate, train, and sustain a values-based culture. These "values champions" worked over the course of a year to create an Andesa Forever booklet—a corporate code of conduct, if you will. For each value, the team provided a definition and synonyms to clarify the definition and questions for self-reflection, so each employee could assess their success in living the value. In addition, a situational awareness behavior description was developed to provide real-life examples of what an employee might encounter with three alternative responses to those situations—one marked red (an inappropriate response), one marked yellow (a marginally appropriate response) and one marked green (an appropriate response). The goal is to drive more and more employees to consistent green behaviors and responses.

Just because a person has values doesn't mean they will abide by them in every encounter and in every situation. Daily pressures, busyness, and stress are the biggest challenges to act in concert with our values, yet these circumstances are the times when we most need to rely on those values. So while the Andesa Forever booklet is used in onboarding and as part of our mentoring program, we incorporate other mechanisms that reinforce the values.

Our High-Five program is peer-to-peer recognition. When an employee observes another employee living the values—a thank you "hand" is provided with a note. At the end of a quarter, employees submit their "hands" to be entered into a raffle for a prize. In addition, we periodically highlight a value focus month where our internal communications emphasize a value, what it looks like in action and how it reinforces our commitment to the value. And, as mentioned earlier, we will soon recognize a values-based employee-owner annually with the John Walker Award.

Every new hire at Andesa visits with each leader in the company over the course of their first ninety days. Yes, you read that right: *Every new hire* meets with *every leader*. Doing so allows them to learn more about the business, the scope of the company, and, of course, the values of the company.

Our values meet our purpose when it comes to our mentorship and training programs. Values training is much deeper than a slide in an onboarding presentation by human resources. Our values champions talk to new hires about the values. An employee-owner-led team developed a mentoring program whereby all new hires are paired with an individual outside of their department. There are few occasions in life that allow us to share our gifts in positively impacting another individual. Mentoring is one of those opportunities. While a leader has the responsibility for the development of the tasks, skills, and responsibilities of the employee's role, a mentor is more of a coach who assists with personal and professional development. Values conversations are a critical component of a mentor-mentee relationship at Andesa.

Recently, I witnessed our experienced analysts teaching, coaching, and imparting the values and culture through their interactions with two new hires whose offices just happened to be outside my office. Most new employees at Andesa learn their job by observing others performing theirs. Approximately 80 percent of employee training involves on-the-job efforts. The experience is fundamentally social and affords the opportunity to transmit Andesa's values and culture—one on one—in such a way that no leader, CEO, book, or training video could ever do as effectively.

In 2019, we also implemented LinkedIn Learning to provide their collection of online professional training content to all employees of Andesa as an employee benefit. Many companies would look at time spent on growth opportunities such as onboarding, training, and development as an expense. But Andesa views employee-owners in human terms, not as an expense line item in a budget. Our purpose is to help our employee-owners and our clients reach their full potential. An investment in an employee-owner is an investment in success for both the individual and the organization. Andesa is willing to invest significant time, talent, and money in the selection and development of employees because we expect employees to stay, grow, and reach their potential throughout their careers with Andesa. Of course, not all stay, but that assumption informs our overall approach to employee investment.

The reality is that, from a client's perspective, the people providing the service are Andesa. Andesa and its clients both benefit from the long-term, loyal staff members who know how to solve our clients' problems and create the Andesa service experience. After a recent client training session, a vice president at the client shared with us that the interaction with our employee-owners "confirmed why we thought the decision to move all products onto this platform was best for our company."

One of the most successful tools we have available to encourage our employee-owners to reach their full potential is the opportunity to participate in a variety of cross-functional teams. Over the course of the past few years, employee teams have tackled some key corporate issues such as a comprehensive compensation and benefits review; development of a continuous quality-improvement program; development of our mentoring program; participation in a diversity, equity, and inclusivity review; engagement activities; employee communications; and our 2020–2025 strategic planning efforts, to name a few.

These teams provide employees the opportunity to take on new responsibilities and leadership roles in meaningful efforts that advance the corporation and provide individual growth opportunities. It is very rewarding to witness the transformation that occurs as participants are provided information and training, then take the initiative and assume responsibility. Similar growth occurs in our client project work and client service teams as individuals grow in confidence through training and experience. Our environment welcomes this progression and rewards the self-starter with increased autonomy and authority.

Our latest employee team is our BAFLE team, which stands for "business acumen, financial literacy, and ESOP" (we love our acronyms at Andesa). This team's challenge is to design education programs to help understand the ESOP and the company's financials. Its efforts are meant to prepare the company for an open-book management future where the employees understand how what they do impacts the financials and the value of the company. And it is a good example of where we can see the shift from maintaining the team to sustaining the team for the long term.

Sustaining the Team—Employee Ownership and Succession Planning

I am a huge proponent of employee ownership as a terrific model for capitalism—because it works for everyone involved. According to statistics from the National Center for Employee Ownership, employee-owned companies outperform their non-employee-owned counterparts when it comes to sales growth, employee retention, loan default rates, and survivability. Recent research concluded that individual employee-owners have 92 percent higher median household wealth, 33 percent higher income from wages, and 53 percent longer median job tenure relative to workers who are not employee-owners. Our move to the ESOP was a financial commitment to our employees to reward their performance in alignment with sustaining our long-term vision.

> Employee-owned companies outperform their non-employee-owned counterparts when it comes to sales growth, employee retention, loan default rates, and survivability.

While Andesa has always had a positive and collaborative environment, I've been encouraged by a noticeable shift of mindset since the 100 percent ESOP transaction was finalized. One of our younger employee-owners perhaps said it best when he recently posted, "I've long been an advocate for bringing unions back. After working at an employee-owned company for over two years now, I can say with certainty that employee-owned is arguably even better than having a unionized position."

The ESOP creates a "we" mentality and rewards employee engagement. A successful company must create an environment that encourages active alignment with its purpose. Not only does it make for good teamwork, but it is recognition that a portion of "my retirement" is going to be supported by the long-term success of the business. When I retire, those still adding value to our clients and each other will repurchase my shares. As they retire, future employees will repurchase their shares. Employee ownership is a catalyst for a long-term, sustainable, privately held business with governance and control held by those who add value to the organization.

That leads us to the importance of succession planning in sustaining the ecosystem. Companies are most vulnerable during leadership transitions. In sports, it is often said that you don't want to be the coach that follows a legendary coach, you want to be the second coach. This is because it is hard for the players and fans to support the new coach in the wake of a fabled leader. When you assume the mantle of leadership, everyone is watching. They are waiting to see how the new leader will react the first time there is a challenge or setback. How are things going to be different? It takes longer than a couple of weeks or months for the cultural transition to occur.

To minimize this risk, I am currently coaching and developing three individuals on my senior leadership team for possible CEO succession at Andesa. And as our ecosystem grows, there may be more. I am transparent in this, and each person is aware of the process. Each has different experiences and different skills, so we tailor their development plan to provide opportunities to round out their leadership exposures. When I retire, my hope is there will be at least three candidates who could lead the company into the future. I will have done my job effectively if the decision is a difficult one for the board to make. Regardless of the outcome, keeping those individuals engaged at Andesa and supporting one another would be the best possible outcome. Each will have advanced their personal and professional resume such that they will be better executives with broader knowledge and broader experience, exactly what the company will need to sustain success.

Personal development work, in alignment with our purpose, is shared among a broader leadership group too. That investment is meant to ensure that the purpose and successful leadership behaviors are fostered across generations of leaders and do not disappear as individuals retire and leave the organization. As we navigated the successful tenures of long-term Andesa legends Bill Smith, Linda Ellison, and Vince Collier, we did so over an elongated cycle to permit the next generation of leaders to assume responsibilities while those foundational leaders were available and still influencing the organization and impacting their successors.

Andesa has been able to build, maintain, and sustain its culture and values through the ups and downs of the business cycles, leadership transitions, and challenges brought about by company growth over thirty-seven years. The response to our employee-engagement-score gut check caused us to reexamine and solidify our environment. But the Andesa Forever story is still being written. We turn our attention to motivating the company for the long term in our next chapter.

CHAPTER TEN

Motivating for the Long Term

Great leaders set up their organizations to succeed beyond their own lifetimes, and when they do, the benefits—for us, for business and even for the shareholder—are extraordinary.
—Simon Sinek

In offering up some final thoughts about values-based leadership, I'd like to focus on the long game. My life has been blessed by engagement with organizations that have remained relevant for over one hundred years. Albright College, my alma mater, was founded in 1856 and is still educating students of academic promise. I began my career in 1983 as a staff accountant at Ernst & Whinney, better known as Ernst & Young today, and it's still going strong. It might surprise you to know that the founders Alwin Ernst and Arthur Young started their small accounting firms in 1903 and 1906, respectively. My career path has included CFO responsibilities at two faith-based, nonprofit healthcare organizations, St. Joseph Medical Center (founded by the Sisters of St. Francis of Philadelphia in 1873) and Phoebe Ministries (founded in 1903), both of which continue to care for the sick, elderly, and needy in our communities. These are examples of corporations whose purpose makes a positive impact such that their organizations' life spans generations. Longevity and loyalty are significant anchors for me.

Life is not a race, and business is not a game. Business can have a huge impact on society, which comes with tremendous social responsibility whether we choose to acknowledge it or not. It is crucial to understand that there is always more value we can create by being successful and supporting others on their paths. There is always a next step to a larger vision, helping more people and creating lasting impact. When it comes to the long game, it is important to remember the pivotal lesson about motivation for the long game from the bestseller *Who Moved My Cheese?*: the cheese is always moving.

The Andesa Forever Vision is a rallying cry to our employee-owners to build a company that lasts over one hundred years. In a pressure-packed, disruptive, and ever-changing business environment, how arrogant does it sound to think we can create something of value that can benefit so many for so long? Yet that's exactly our quest. The success of my tenure as CEO will not be measured in my lifetime but will be recognized only if I strengthened the foundation established by John Walker and the leaders who came before me. My success will be achieved if Andesa remains a values-based firm that learns, adapts, and makes a positive impact for decades after I'm gone.

On my path to becoming a better leader, I was introduced to Tugboat Institute, headquartered in Sun Valley, Idaho. Tugboat Institute is a membership organization that supports Evergreen

164

leaders and their teams by creating content and experiences that curate members' best practices and wisdom, inspiring leaders in their journey to build enduring private companies.

The Tugboat Institute story is unique. Its founder, Dave Whorton, enjoyed a stellar career as an investor at two of the top venture capital and private equity firms in the world. A transformational conversation in 2005 with Stella & Dot founder Jessica Herrin challenged his beliefs about business. Dave's curiosity led to many more conversations with leaders around the country who were striving to build and grow meaningful companies without the expectation of exit. In 2013, Dave coined the term "Evergreen" to describe the companies and leaders driving this long-game movement.

When I learned of the Evergreen movement, I approached our board of directors about participation with the group as an investment in my leadership. I emailed the Evergreen 7Ps principles to John Walker to seek his support, and he immediately responded with tongue-in-cheek humor: "Have they hacked our emails?" It was instant validation that Andesa's core business beliefs and those of the Tugboat Institute member companies were aligned. In 2020, Andesa was Certified Evergreen in recognition of how Andesa historically operated and continues to do so today.

Participation with Tugboat Institute affords me the opportunity to engage with and learn from like-minded business leaders. As we continue to build Andesa Forever, the opportunity to learn best practices and gain hard-earned wisdom from others has proven invaluable.

The Evergreen 7Ps principles represent the defining characteristics of Evergreen leaders and strategies of Evergreen companies. Let's examine how each principle manifests in the Andesa journey by first sharing our Andesa Forever Vision statement:

ANDESA IS: A 100 percent employee-owned organization, grounded in an ethical culture, which encourages and facilitates its employee-owners to develop and apply their business skills to the fullest, for both client and employee-owner to achieve their full potential.

*Individuals—who thrive on excellence and achievement and who embody the **CORE VALUES** of honesty, respect, integrity, responsibility, courage, and initiative in all they do—are the foundation of Andesa.*

We believe in the worth of the individual and the power of the human spirit. These beliefs motivate our employee-owners to work on behalf of each other, as well as future employee-owners. Each employee-owner accepts the responsibility to leave Andesa in better shape than we found it.

Our quest is to be an outstanding example of an employee-driven company, recognized for our values-based culture, superior workforce, and exemplary services. Our journey requires a long-term, strategic discipline whereby:

- *We must continuously attract, develop, and retain values-based, talented individuals.*

- *We must provide superior value for our clients such that they can exceed their business objectives.*

- *We must carefully pursue target markets, products, and service offerings that provide challenging work and career advancement opportunities for our employee-owners.*

- *We must steadily grow to generate sufficient profits such that we appropriately compensate and reward our employee-owners, afford the resources necessary to maintain very high standards, and can invest in best-practices technology.*

Andesa is the combined strength of a supportive organizational structure and individual talents constantly reinforcing and empowering each other. Andesa is far stronger than the sum of its parts. It is a company making such a positive impact that it has an anticipated FOREVER *life span.*

The Evergreen 7Ps Principles at Andesa

Purpose means being passionately driven by a compelling vision and mission. Understanding our *why* (the purpose, cause, or belief that drives us) is critical to understanding Andesa. We are driven by something much deeper than a paycheck. We believe in the value of the individual. As noted in our vision, our purpose is to help those individuals—our colleagues and our clients—reach their full potential. Can you think of any higher calling? I am blessed to lead an organization whose purpose aligns so well with my personal purpose.

We are driven to make decisions that invest in relationships—with our employee-owners, our teams, and our clients. We are in the relationship business, and we understand that to our core.

We talk about sustaining a culture because we believe in our model, a vision that focuses on finding and hiring quality individuals with good character and then challenging our team to grow as professionals over their career with Andesa. This approach has been a large reason for Andesa's success and will continue to be as we march into the future.

People First means engaging a workforce of talented associates who excel as a team and are motivated by the mission and culture as well as the total compensation, with the belief that by taking care of them, they will take care of the customers, suppliers, partners, communities, and their families.

Our vision requires that we attract, develop and retain values-based individuals who accept the responsibility to leave Andesa better than when they started. We appreciate that the complexity of our industry and systems is best served by developing talent. Throughout its history, Andesa has made decisions that reject the alternative of maintaining the status quo and short-term financial results in favor of investing in people and the long term. If you build the right environment and strive to improve the lives of those who entrust you with their livelihood, you will develop a brand with a bigger sense of purpose than simply maximizing quarterly profits.

> If you build the right environment and strive to improve the lives of those who entrust you with their livelihood, you will develop a brand with a bigger sense of purpose than simply maximizing quarterly profits.

Perseverance means having the resilience to overcome obstacles and to keep pursuing the mission indefinitely into the future. Looking back at thirty-seven-plus years of Andesa history, there have been many stories of heroes and examples of grit, determination, and persistence. The Andesa journey involves some wonderful views from the peaks—but has also required endurance through the valleys. There will always be changes in business models, economic cycles, technologies, programming languages, new leaders, regulations, etc. We believe investment in our employee-owners is the best way for us to persevere for a forever future.

Private means taking advantage of the ability of closely held, private companies to have longer investment horizons, greater confidentiality around strategies, and more operational flexibility than public or exit-oriented businesses. We believe the ESOP is the best economic ownership structure to protect our ability to remain private. It is an investment in our belief of self-governance, which allows us to preserve the employee and client focus with a long-term perspective.

We are not beholden to quarterly earnings calls (or monthly earnings reviews of private-equity-backed companies). We can align our values, culture, and efforts with those of our clients' long-term life insurance products and philosophies. Our clients have trusted us with their systems and administrative processing. We maintain a long-term view when it comes to investing and in our relationships with our clients.

Paced Growth means having the discipline to focus on long-term strategy, balance short-term and long-term performance, and grow steadily and consistently from year to year.

Many publications recognize companies who achieve rapid, year-over-year increases in revenue with a "fastest-growing" moniker. However, such growth can be fleeting. For example, less than 10 percent of the *Inc.* 5000, five thousand of the fastest-growing companies in 2011, were able to earn that recognition for five consecutive years. Only one of the top 25 on the list in 2011 even made the list in 2016—and they came in at number 4,953.

Over the years, Andesa has experienced ups and downs—not a pattern of steady, consistent growth, but when viewed from a long-term perspective, the peaks and valleys reflect steady progress.

That steady progress is essential to success over the long term. It is incumbent upon leadership to live true to the firm's purpose, remain people-first, and ensure the environment continues to "allow people to go where their motivation takes them."

Pragmatic Innovation means embracing a continuous-improvement process built around taking capital-efficient, calculated risks to innovate creatively within constraints.

Pragmatic innovation requires a balance of staying abreast of new technology and determining how core applications fit. Our systems are the result of investments in partnership with our clients. Andesa's relationship managers develop trusted-advisor relationships with our clients to identify new opportunities. Core technology has its own unique profile of functional strengths that new technology can never fully replace. The key to continued success is to improve and integrate the old with the new. Many of our clients will select enterprise-wide digital experiences or data analytics solutions—the exuberance of today's insurtech market. Andesa understands it must "plug and play" into those solutions.

We also understand that, for certain product offerings, our clients will rely on Andesa for those same broad digital capabilities and experiences. Andesa must also offer a full set of solutions to meet those needs as well, whether built by us or offered through partnerships. One thing is for sure: we will continue to be driven by our belief in pragmatic innovation.

Profit is essential to survival and independence and the most accurate measure of customer value being delivered—but it's not the purpose of the business. Andesa has a healthy perspective on profitability. Looking back, a company doesn't get to celebrate thirty-seven years in business without understanding how profit fuels investments over time. That being said, we don't take our past success for granted.

Each employee-owner understands our financial goals and potential obstacles. Team members closest to the work have maximum impact on the business. This will be especially important and rewarding as we refine our ESOP culture, where sweat equity results in retirement account growth.

As we plan our path forward, we will continue to strive for the ability to reinvest in our culture, our people, and our systems. Doing so is the best way to ensure our future. A strong, healthy Andesa is the best way for our clients to avoid issues and risks with services and systems.

Motivation 3.0

In creating the environment for the long term, a leader's objective is to make everyone around them better. Everything hinges on the leader's relationship to the individuals associated with the organization. Does the leader control or inspire?

In his 2009 bestseller *Drive: The Surprising Truth about What Motivates Us*, author Daniel Pink introduces us to the leadership philosophy of Motivation 3.0. According to Pink, "The aims of these Motivation 3.0 companies are not to chase profit while trying to stay ethical and law-abiding. Their goal is to pursue purpose and to use profit as the catalyst rather than the objective." Pink further notes, "Motivation 3.0 doesn't reject profits, but places equal emphasis on purpose maximization."

Pink goes on to note that "human beings have an innate inner drive to be autonomous, self-determined, and connected to one another. And when the drive is liberated, people achieve more and live richer lives."[23]

---

23 Daniel H. Pink, *Drive: The Surprising Truth about What Motivates Us* (New York: Riverhead Books, 2009).

Values-based leaders eschew "carrot and stick" coercion, seeking to ignite intrinsic motivation with an appeal to the heart. Values-based leaders tap into ideals such as respect, integrity, courage, honesty, initiative, and responsibility to rouse the spirit. They attempt to align an individual's purpose and talents with an organization's needs and objectives. Creating environments that allow an employee-owner to succeed helps them and the organization approach their full potential. The pride and engagement stirred through intrinsic motivation leads to a sense of ownership. It is why you should focus on doing business with those who believe in what you believe. When an individual's values and purpose align with their company's values and purpose, and those align with the ecosystem in which the individuals and company operates, that person's soul sings, and they will make a difference. Leadership is about creating such an environment and alignment.

Many of us spend most of our waking hours engaged in our chosen employment. I strive to spend my time leading a life of meaning, supporting others on their journey to reach their potential. Each of us must find meaning in our work if we are to remain inspired over the long term. For Andesa to be successful in the long run, the company must continue to find and retain values-based individuals who are committed to each other and our clients as well as aligned with our company's purpose.

> Each of us must find meaning in our work if we are to remain inspired over the long term.

Through my transition from CPA to CFO to CEO, I uncovered my purpose of helping others—my personal Motivation 3.0, if you will. Today, I draw inspiration from many conversations with Andesa staff and from our clients. When a teammate appreciates the environment and their personal growth results, when they are energized by their journey, it provides the proof that I am making a difference and fuels my drive to keep going.

A Call to Values-Based Leadership

Gallup surveys repeatedly report that nearly twenty percent of US workers perform below their potential. According to estimates, this translates to approximately $300 billion of lost productivity and opportunity annually. These surveys only measure the individual's potential within their current role in the business and miss the multiplier effect if the individual was consistently learning and growing. When Andesa emphasizes our purpose to encourage our employee-owners to achieve their full potential, it is a much greater calling than improving their performance in their role or their perceived value to the business. It's about making a difference and an impact with those we bring aboard. It is respect for them as individuals combined with the honesty, courage, initiative, responsibility, and integrity to make a difference and a commitment to do so for the long term—in other words, Andesa Forever.

The world needs values-based leaders dedicated to improving the lives of those they lead; self-aware leaders with a strong commitment to core values, who live and impart them to future generations; leaders with a core sense of purpose who draw others to that mission; leaders dedicated to a cause bigger than themselves, who put people first; leaders who set up their missions and organizations to succeed beyond their own lifetimes and who persevere through the ups and downs to see their vision have lasting impact.

John Walker's vision and leadership of Andesa inspired and transformed me from a "results first, people second" leader to a values-based, people-first leader.

The business world all too often measures leadership success based upon results, but in the end, a leader can't motivate numbers. Leadership is about people. Leaders are responsible for the people who produce the results. It's not about measurement but about motivation. It's been a long journey for this accountant to appreciate that the true measure of success of the corporation isn't the income statement and balance sheet. The desire for high performance comes from within those you lead. Your role as a leader is to create the environment to encourage and nurture this intrinsic desire for success.

Love Your Work

Finally, I hope from your reading journey with me you can tell that I love my work, I love my colleagues at Andesa, and I love the clients with whom we partner to build a special ecosystem. We've all heard the business guru motivation, "If you love what you do, you will never work a day in your life." Even though I love it, it is not easy. Work is work. It requires a lot of stamina and emotional stability to persevere.

From my perspective, leadership is a constant growth journey, one that I do truly love. Speaking of LOVE, allow me to leave you with an acronym to guide your values-based leadership journey:

Look inward.

Obsess over learning.

Volunteer.

Eliminate "head trash."

Look inward: Self-awareness is a critical element of your personal and professional growth journey. Growth comes from recognizing your passion and skills while eliminating those things that do not advance you. Challenging times offer opportunity for growth and provide affirmation of that growth. Embrace the challenges, step outside your comfort zone, and keep growing.

- Advice to values-based leaders: Pay it forward. As you grow and learn more about yourself, you serve your team better when you seek to understand your team and encourage them to transform themselves. Helping someone uncover a hidden talent is highly rewarding. Coaching, mentoring, and regular conversations about the work, the business needs, and the individual's personal passions may provide a tremendous opportunity for their growth.

Obsess over learning: Leaders learn. Create space in your life for learning and growth. Stay curious. Engage in dialogue and debate. Lead with questions. Read books; read articles; watch videos. Networking provides tremendous opportunities to learn new ideas. Whatever your mode for learning, dedicate time to the process of personal growth.

- Advice to values-based leaders: In your leadership role, provide an environment that encourages questions and departmental mentoring. Formal training can help, but challenging high performers to fail and figure things out can provide an even greater learning environment. Encourage such an environment.

Volunteer: Be proactive in your own growth. Be open to new challenges; be eager to figure things out. Remember the mantra "Growth occurs outside your comfort zone," and show the courage to embrace taking the initiative. Perform in your role, but when provided the opportunity, jump at the chance to say yes and figure it out.

- Advice to values-based leaders: Create an environment that provides opportunities but allows individuals to struggle with challenges.

Eliminate "head trash": Everyone has self-doubt as they travel their growth journey. How does a leader overcome self-doubt or nagging negativity? Serve others. It's not about you, it's about the people and the bigger organization.

- Advice to values-based leaders: I have often found an employee's intrinsic motivation sets a higher bar than I would have set for that individual. Engage your team with setting their own goals, provide support—then stand back! A leader who provides opportunity for a colleague to pursue a challenging task demonstrates their belief and trust in the individual. Don't be afraid to set high expectations; high performers will seek to reach them.

Look inward, **O**bsess over learning, **V**olunteer, and **E**liminate head trash. **LOVE** the process, and you will love what the process produces. I wish you the best on your values-based leadership journey.

ACKNOWLEDGMENTS

As an avid reader, I now have a greater appreciation for the labor of the author through the writer's journey.

Thank you to my friends, family, and colleagues on this writing journey who inspired me, endured conversations about the book, and read and provided feedback. Vince Collier, this book is certainly better and my message about values and ecosystems more clearly expressed because of your friendship and support.

To the entire team at Advantage Media Group, I am grateful for your guidance, teamwork, support, encouragement, and assistance with publishing. Special appreciation to Regina Roths and Jenny Tripp, who challenged me and believed there was a story worth telling. I am ever grateful for your collaboration.

I am humbled and honored that my friends would submit "Voices of the Industry" reflections to this effort. Your words testify to the importance of the alignment of personal values to our work and our industry's ecosystem. I am blessed to serve and work alongside you in this noble field.

And finally, thank you, the reader, for investing your valuable time to read this story.

ABOUT THE AUTHOR

As president and CEO of Andesa Services Inc., Ron is responsible for guiding Andesa toward its strategic goals. Ron's life and business journey led him to understand the importance of a purpose-driven and people-first culture in building and operating a successful business. He is motivated to help and encourage people to find and maximize their purpose to make a positive impact on the world. He is a CPA with a bachelor's degree in accounting from Albright College, where he serves as the chair of the college's board of trustees.

Printed in the USA
CPSIA information can be obtained
at www.ICGtesting.com
JSHW012031140824
68134JS00033B/2989